T0301350

Entrepreneurship and the Financial Community

Entrepreneurship and the Financial Community

Starting Up and Growing New Businesses

Edited by

Bart Clarysse

Professor of Innovation and Technology Management, Vlerick Leuven Ghent Management School and Ghent University, Ghent, Belgium

Juan Roure

Professor of Entrepreneurship, IESE Business School, University of Navarra, Barcelona, Spain

Tom Schamp

Advisor European Programmes, Institute for the Promotion of Innovation through Science and Technology Flanders (IWT) Brussels, Belgium

IN ASSOCIATION WITH GATE2GROWTH ACADEMIC NETWORK, EUROPEAN COMMISSION – DG ENTERPRISE AND INDUSTRY

Edward Elgar

Cheltenham, UK • Northampton, MA, USA

Published by
Edward Elgar Publishing Limited
Glensanda House
Montpellier Parade
Cheltenham
Glos GL50 1UA
UK

Edward Elgar Publishing, Inc.
William Pratt House
9 Dewey Court
Northampton
Massachusetts 01060
USA

A catalogue record for this book
is available from the British Library

Library of Congress Cataloguing in Publication Data
Entrepreneurship and the financial community : starting up and growing new businesses / edited by Bart Clarysse, Juan Roure, Tom Schamp.
    p.   cm.
Includes bibliographical references and index.
1. Venture capital.   2. New business enterprises — Finance.   3.
Entrepreneurship.   I. Clarysse, Bart, 1969–   II. Roure, Juan B.   III. Schamp, Tom, 1971–

HG4751.E584   2006
    658.15′224 — dc22

2006017827

ISBN 978 1 84542 647 7 (cased)

Printed and bound in Great Britain by MPG Books Ltd, Bodmin, Cornwall

Contents

Contributors

Rudy Aernoudt Policy Unit of the Ministry of Economy, Energy, Foreign Trade and Science, Brussels, Belgium.

Richard P. Bagozzi University of Michigan, Ann Arbor, MI, USA.

Simon Barnes Tanaka Business School, Imperial College London, UK.

Massimo Bergami Alma Mater Studiorum, Università di Bologna, Italy.

Christof Beuselinck Department of Accounting and Corporate Finance, Ghent University, Belgium.

Reinhard Büscher European Commission, Directorate General Enterprise and Industry – Innovation Policy Unit, Brussels, Belgium.

Bart Clarysse Operations and Technology Management Centre (OTMC), Vlerick Leuven Ghent Management School, Belgium.

Dirk De Clercq Faculty of Business, Brock University, Ontario, Canada.

Christian Diller Center for Entrepreneurial and Financial Studies (CEFS), Department of Financial Management and Capital Markets, Technische Universität München, Germany.

Dimo Dimov School of Business, Department of Management, University of Connecticut, Storrs, CT, USA.

Vance H. Fried Willam S. Spears School of Business, Oklahoma State University, Stillwater, OK, USA.

Richard T. Harrison University of Edinburgh Management School, UK.

Teresa Hogan Dublin City University Business School, Ireland.

Elaine Hutson University College Dublin, Ireland.

Christoph Kaserer Center for Entrepreneurial and Financial Studies (CEFS), Department of Financial Management and Capital Markets, Technische Universität München, Germany.

Mirjam Knockaert Operations and Technology Management Centre (OTMC), Vlerick Leuven Ghent Management School, Belgium.

Claire M. Leitch   School of Management & Economics, Queen's University, Belfast, UK.

Andy Lockett   Centre for Management Buy-Out Research (CMBOR), Nottingham University Business School, UK.

Markus M. Mäkelä   Department of Information Technology, University of Turku, Turku, Finland.

Sophie Manigart   Department of Accounting and Corporate Finance, Ghent University, Belgium.

Markku V.J. Maula   Institute of Strategy and International Business, Helsinki University of Technology (HUT), Finland.

Vanessa Menzies   Allianz Private Equity UK Holdings, London, UK.

Gabriele Morandin   Alma Mater Studiorum, Università di Bologna, Italy.

Gordon Murray   School of Business & Economics, University of Exeter, UK.

Juan Roure   Department of Entrepreneurship, IESE Business School, University of Navarra, Barcelona, Spain.

Amparo de San José Riestra   Department of Entrepreneurship, IESE Business School, University of Navarra, Barcelona, Spain.

Tom Schamp   Gate2Growth Academic Network in Entrepreneurship, Innovation and Finance – European Institute for Advanced Studies in Management (EIASM), and Advisor European Programmes, IWT Flanders, Brussels, Belgium.

Tom Van Cauwenberge   Deloitte Touche Tohmatsu, Diegem, Belgium.

Caroline Van Eeckhout   Operations and Technology Management Centre (OTMC), Vlerick Leuven Ghent Management School, Belgium.

Mike Wright   Centre for Management Buy-Out Research (CMBOR), Nottingham University Business School, UK.

About the editors

Bart Clarysse holds a PhD in applied economics from Ghent University (1996). He is a Professor of Innovation and Technology Management at Vlerick Leuven Ghent Management School and at Ghent University (Ghent, Belgium). He has carried out various projects concerning technology management for national and international organizations such as OECD, IWT (Vlaams Instituut voor de Aanmoediging van Innovatie door Wetenschap en Technologie), the European Commission, and has published internationally in this domain. Since 1998, he has been a scientific adviser for the IWT with regard to Flemish innovation and technology policy. He was also involved in the start-up of several high-tech companies. He has written several international publications in the field of R&D management and technology policy in journals such as *Entrepreneurship Theory and Practice, Journal of Business Venturing, Research Policy, International Journal of Technology Management* and *Science Technology and Industry Review*. Dr Clarysse is the Scientific Director of the Gate2Growth Academic Network in Entrepreneurship, Innovation and Finance.

Juan Roure is Professor of Entrepreneurship at the IESE Business School (University of Navarra, Barcelona, Spain). His areas of interest include innovation, entrepreneurship and new ventures, strategy and negotiation as a management process. Dr Roure holds a PhD in engineering management from Stanford University (USA), an MBA from ESADE (Spain), a degree in industrial engineering from the Polytechnic University of Cataluña (Spain), and an Individual Study Project (IPS) from the Graduate School of Business Administration, Harvard University (USA).

Tom Schamp is Advisor European Programmes at IWT Flanders (Brussels, Belgium). From June 2002 to August 2006, Mr Schamp was the manager of the Gate2Growth Academic Network in Entrepreneurship, Innovation and Finance, on behalf of the European Institute for Advanced Studies in Management (EIASM, Brussels, Belgium). From 1999 to 2002, Mr Schamp was a senior researcher at the Faculty of Economics and Business Administration, Ghent University (Belgium). From 1996 to 1999 he was a research assistant at the SME Department and the Centre for Entrepreneurship at the Vlerick Leuven Ghent Management School

(VLGMS, Belgium). His main research interests are start-ups, strategy and strategic planning, and the development and growth of high-tech companies. Mr Schamp has obtained degrees in political sciences and international relations, and a MaM in applied developmental economics.

Preface and acknowledgements

The Gate2Growth Academic Network in Entrepreneurship, Innovation and Finance was launched in the summer of 2002 as a part of the Gate2Growth Initiative (www.gate2growth.com), which is sponsored by the European Commission's Innovation Policy Unit (DG Enterprise and Industry), under the Fifth Framework Programme 'SME and Innovation' (FP5). The European Institute for Advanced Studies in Management (www.eiasm.org) and the Vlerick Leuven Ghent Management School (www.vlerick.be) drew on their respective strengths and ambitions to coordinate and run the G2G Academic Network. (Note: until the change of the name in 2004 the network was called Gate2Growth Finance Academia.)

The main objectives of the G2G Academic Network in Entrepreneurship, Innovation and Finance are:

1. to foster the development of the academic profession, essentially research and teaching in entrepreneurship, innovation and finance;
2. to support the exchange, dissemination and integration of knowledge, research expertise and teaching practice on a pan-European scale; and
3. to filter from the data, insights and results of the different activities conclusions, recommendations and guidelines that can help policy making, foremost at the European Commission.

The most essential activities and deliverables are the doctoral seminar series (PhD research papers), the specialized research workshops (proceedings and handbook publications, for example, this volume), the exchange and mobility of researchers (setting up an exchange directory, working papers etc.), the European case competition (teaching case portfolios), and the annual European best paper award competition.

Ever since the start of the project these activities have made the network an important point of reference for the support, generation and dissemination of top-level academic research expertise at the earliest possible stage and of good teaching practice in the three main research domains. As more fundamental research results are translated into more practical insights and the development of specific training formats (toolkit), the findings and other deliverables are disseminated to a wider audience, including policy makers and the business world. In an effort to centralize and share on a pan-European scale the largely fragmented knowledge and expertise, the network has become a prime partner for the European Community (EC) in many different ways. First of all, the network actively helps to formulate policy guidelines and policy recommendations to stimulate entrepreneurial activity, and to detect better ways of supporting and financing innovative start-ups or research-based and high-tech ventures. Second, via the activities the network intends to increase the amount and quality of entrepreneurship research and education, as well as the educational impact of courses in entrepreneurship, innovation and finance. Also, the network facilitates the development of proper tools and methodologies of use for the various interested parties, that is, business owners, politicians, investors, academics and other innovation experts and professionals.

At the time of the first specialized research workshop (SRW), the papers of which were the foundation for this publication, the network numbered over 170 members, that is, researchers and professors in entrepreneurship, innovation and finance. At the time, close to 75 academic institutions from all 25 EU countries were involved in its activities. Today the network comprises some 300 members of close to 200 different research and knowledge institutions Europe wide.

As we have said already, the goal of the G2G Academic Network is to facilitate the exchange of knowledge and experience and to stimulate collaboration among European academia in the field of entrepreneurship and to channel this knowledge towards European policy makers. One of the more prominent activities sponsored under the programme is the yearly SRW. The key aspect of all papers accepted for the SRW is that they focus on issues associated with stimulating entrepreneurship and innovation and the financing aspects of emerging and growing companies. This book represents the proceedings of the First Specialized Research Workshop on 'Managing Growth: The Role of Private Equity' hosted by the IESE Business School (University of Navarra, Barcelona, Spain: 12 November 2004). The topic of the workshop was the role of private equity in achieving and managing growth of new businesses, hence the title of this book. For more than a decade, venture capital has been promoted as an engine for growth and technological innovation, worldwide. Venture capitalists are not only finance providers; it is widely understood that they also contribute to value creation in the companies in which they invest. Venture capital-backed companies – although the empirical findings are open to discussion – seem to grow faster in terms of number of jobs created, their sales or profits. For these reasons the role of venture capital firms in the promotion of technology-based ventures has received considerable attention from the business world, researchers and policy makers.

Among the guidelines used by those selecting the papers for presentation and publication was that research should mirror issues in the field of venture capital in the context of the financing and growth of entrepreneurial firms. Both the research and the methodology should be novel and sound and the conference theme approached from a different angle. Findings should be relevant for European companies, investors and policy makers. As a result, 12 of the 13 contributions selected for this book emanate from researchers from all over Europe (seven different countries) and study phenomena at a local and a European level. Chapter 13 then examines good practices and policy recommendations.

I thank the IESE Business School for their hospitality and for hosting the workshop. I also express my gratitude to the participants for formulating their many important questions and for sharing their precise and critical viewpoints. My gratitude and respect also goes to the invited speakers and distinguished contributors of this book, the members of the working group managing the scientific and academic requirements of the workshop (that is, Dr Margarida Fontes (Instituto Nacional de Engenhana, Tecnologia e Inovação (INETI), Lisbon, Portugal), Dr Loïc Mahérault (EM Lyon, France), Dr Massimo Colombo (Politechnico di Milano, Italy), Dr Philippe Mustar (Ecoles des Mines de Paris, France) and Dr Marco van Gelderen (Erasmus Universiteit, Rotterdam, Netherlands)), as well as the members of the G2G Academic Network board of directors (that is, Dr Mike Wright (Nottingham University Business School, UK), Dr Sophie Manigart (Universiteit Gent, Belgium), Dr Jean Bonnet (University of Caen, France), Dr Hans Landström (University of Lund, Sweden) and Dr Bart Clarysse (Vlerick Leuven Ghent Management School, Belgium), the Scientific Director of the G2G Academic Network.

The book attempts to reflect the multiplicity of stakeholders and relationships existing in the venture capital ecosystem. Some authors examine, for instance, technical factors routing private equity (for example, fundraising mechanisms from the institutional fund providers' side, how to better measure venture capital fund performance, the selection criteria of venture capitalists in the early-stage segment, and also, how to increase the angel investors' base in Europe). Other authors examine more human factors involved (for example, the motivation of entrepreneurs to use venture capital, the impact of venture capitalists for instance on dealing with internationalization, and the importance of establishing good relationships with investors to maximize benefits. Finally the book includes some contributions reviewing the specific problematic of university spin-outs and the well-known equity gap phenomenon.

Our journey into the unique world of European private equity and venture capital holders ready to support the creation and growth of new businesses, however, begins with the onset of the venture capital investment cycle – insights from institutions providing funds to venture capitalists – and ends with a fresh revision of the equity gap in the early-stage segment. In between these chapters, the reader will find contributions on specific elements of the venture capital cycle.

Tom Schamp
Brussels, March 2006

Foreword

The objective of European innovation policy is to facilitate networking among the main drivers for innovation in Europe and to further develop innovation policies in support of enterprises. The activities of the General Directorate Enterprise and Industry in the area of innovation and entrepreneurship are designed to create favourable conditions for making innovation happen. The most recent initiative is Europe INNOVA, which aims at bringing together industrial innovation stakeholders with finance in order to assist young innovative enterprises in their efforts to develop new markets and to grow faster.

Europe INNOVA builds on the successful Gate2Growth Initiative (2002–2006: www.gate2growth.com) which aims 'to provide access to private innovation financing and tools for better knowledge exploitation'. The initiative focuses on helping important support players to improve their capacity to assist entrepreneurs by networking and exchanging experience and good practice at the European level. These include early-stage technology venture capital investors, managers of technology incubators, managers of industrial liaison and technology transfer offices linked to universities, business schools and other specialized research centres, academics in entrepreneurship, innovation and finance research and teaching. Gate2Growth thus provides the tools, infrastructure and support services directed to innovative entrepreneurs as well as to their supporters.

Now that Gate2Growth is drawing to a close there is clear evidence showing that the ultimate objective of this initiative, namely to support the innovative entrepreneurs in Europe, has been met. Many players have contributed to this success. Besides the organization of partnering events between innovators and investors, a better understanding of existing barriers to finance has contributed to the success of this initiative. There is not only a lack of risk capital in Europe but also a lack of entrepreneurial innovation management capabilities that prevents early-stage finance and venture capital markets from developing more quickly.

Statistics are not enough to fully capture the specificities and dynamics of risk capital in Europe. To properly address innovation policy challenges a deeper understanding of the underlying factors that explain why innovation performance in Europe is still suboptimal is urgently needed. The

book here presented is a model for the way in which academia has contributed to the knowledge and understanding of finance mechanisms in
support of entrepreneurial innovation and venturing.

We wish you a very pleasant read!

Reinhard Büscher
European Commission, DG Enterprise
and Industry, Innovation Policy

Introduction

1. INTRODUCTION

1.1 Relevance

As we move into the goals of the Lisbon Strategy of mobilizing and exchanging the knowledge and good practice of academia and industry, the role of entrepreneurship, innovation and the financing of such activities becomes more important. The objective is no longer reduced to fostering the creation of new and technology-based firms, but to make these firms grow to be able to compete in the European and global market. Central to achieving this goal is the issue of how to transfer technology from universities to the market, how to manage professionally these new firms, and how to facilitate growth processes within these firms.

1.2 Context and Objective

Researchers in the area of entrepreneurship and innovation often come from different academic disciplines and there is no instrument that ensures the dissemination of their findings to other interested parties, in particular to policy makers. The organization of specialized research workshops and the publication of the workshop proceedings facilitate the exchange of knowledge in the entrepreneurship field and channel this knowledge towards European politicians, more in particular the European Commission's DG Enterprise and Industry.

The central theme for this research workshop was 'Managing growth: the role of private equity'. The objective of the specialized research workshop is to collect the insights of leading academics and researchers on the subject; in casu to promote a better understanding of the role of private equity providers in the development of growth-oriented start-ups and the management of growth processes.

The purpose of this book is to translate the body of scientific and fundamental knowledge that was presented at the workshop into more practice-oriented findings and papers, which are useful for the larger G2G community including investors, entrepreneurs, business owners, policy makers and academia.

Contributions were selected through a three-stage review process (abstract, 2000 word summary and full paper). In total more than 40 proposals were submitted in this highly specialized field of venture finance, high-tech start-ups and growth. In the end 12 papers were selected and distributed over three different streams, each one of them illuminating a different perspective on the role and relevance of private equity for starting and growing new ventures: 'the venture capitalist's perspective', 'the entrepreneur's perspective' and 'the role of government'. At the end of the workshop, three papers received a 2004 European Best Paper Award (an activity also funded by the Gate2Growth Academic Network): Clarysse, B., Knockaert, M. and Lockett A., 'How do early stage high technology investors select their investments?' (First Rank), Murray, G. and Dimov, D., 'Through a glass darkly: new perspectives on the equity gap' (Second Rank), and Lockett, A. and Wright, M., 'Resources, capabilities, risk capital and the creation of university spin-out companies' (Third Rank). The review and selection of the best papers was based on more than 20 different parameters, including the level of contribution to the body of knowledge on the topic, the soundness of the research methodology and the newness, importance and significance of the research findings, in particular with respect to the EC. Also, the research is post-doctoral in nature and has not yet been published or accepted for publication by any journal or book publisher.

2. ENTREPRENEURSHIP AND THE FINANCIAL COMMUNITY

In the introduction we want to highlight the importance of the topic and give a more general description of the evolution of the venture capital industry. The main argument is that in the early 1990s, practitioners in the industry pointed out screening and analysis of opportunities as their main competitive advantage. Today, they see themselves as hands-on investors capable of delivering value added. But do they really add value? This book has three main parts, each part representing new research findings relating to one specific perspective on the role of private equity in managing start-ups and firm growth.

2.1 Part I: The Financial Community's Perspective on the Role of Private Equity

Financial institutions, corporations and wealthy individuals are at the origin of the supply side of the venture capital and private equity market.

Although venture capital might represent only a small percentage of an overall assets portfolio, private investors are aware that superior returns will be obtained only if they successfully cherry-pick the best investment teams in the market.

In Chapter 1, Barnes and Menzies show how limited partners follow clear procedures for managing the annual allocation of capital to venture capital as an asset class. The authors demonstrate that investors use different selection methods which can be either subjective or objective.

According to the authors, the process followed by investors to select funds can be broken down into various stages. The process starts with two types of screening. In the initial screening investors revise the document-ation of the fund, while in the following screening stage personal, but infor-mal, meetings with venture capitalists (VCs) take place. The selection criteria at the overall screening stage are magnitude and consistence of returns, top quartile returns, limited partners (LPs) diversification strategy, and value-adding capacity of general partners (GPs). These screening steps are followed by a process of ratification, in which the investors carry out intense due diligence. The process ends with the evaluation stage, when investors select the funds where they will invest. The main criteria applied for this selection are: experience, stability and homogeneity of the team, the track record of the team, consistency of the strategy proposed with previ-ous experience of the same team, and fund terms.

One of the observations is that the team of LP analysts builds consensus on the selected funds early in the process, in particular at the ratification stage. LP analysts appear to track and then back a core group of VCs with whom they develop long-term relationships. For this reason, new venture capital teams encounter special difficulties to raise funds, as many investors have made their decision before these new VCs approach them.

In Chapter 2, Clarysse et al. bring some novel insights into the long period between fundraising and exit. Considering the debate as to whether venture capitalists generate superior returns from their selection, deal structuring or added-value capabilities, the chapter investigates the invest-ment decisions of early-stage VCs. In particular the authors analyse how venture capital managers select their investments, what selection criteria they apply and what factors influence different selection behaviour observed. The authors present four dimensions decisive to the investment decision, namely, team, market, product and financing methods. According to the relevance that different investors attach to these four criteria, the results of the chapter indicate the raising of three major types of investors. They group these investors into 'technology' investors, 'people' investors, and 'financial' investors and rank the main investment criteria differently.

According to the authors, investors in the first group focus primarily on protectability and uniqueness of the technology and the relationship that can be established with the entrepreneur/s. The team characteristics are not that important for them. These VC funds have managers with strong technical profiles. The second group, people investors, place their emphasis on human capital factors while protectability of technology is considered less important. Investment managers in the group of financial investors focus heavily on the potential returns expected from the business proposals. The last group of investors identified requires a well-built team, whose members must be experienced and complementary; in the absence of these, it will be difficult to raise capital from financial investors.

Continuing with the value creation process for their LP base, venture capital investors contribute to the companies where they invest in different ways. Among others, these investors use extensive monitoring devices to control and follow up their portfolio firms. In Chapter 3, Beuselinck et al. approach unsolved questions as to how private equity investors monitor and control their portfolio firms and to what extent these efforts influence the corporate governance system in place in the companies. The authors also research to what extent private equity investors' involvement affects their portfolio firm's further development and professionalization.

The research carried out by Beuselinck et al. distinguishes Anglo-Saxon from continental investors with respect to the frequency and intensity of their monitoring and communication practices with investees. They suggest that it is more common for Anglo-Saxon investors to appoint a representative to the board. And meetings of this board are more frequent in companies backed by these investors. The authors also prove that for Anglo-Saxon investors the information reported by companies to fund managers is identical to the information that these sent to the board, which is not the case for continental ones (perhaps because board meetings are less frequent). *Ad hoc* contact is more frequent with Anglo-Saxon investors, and it encompasses a broader number of firm directors (other than the chief executive officer (CEO) and the chief financial officer (CFO) for continental investors). A final, but equally important contribution of this chapter is the presentation of the impact of private equity monitoring and control on the portfolio firms' financial reporting, that is, considering the extent of earnings management, earnings conservatism and disclosure of information as indicators of financial reporting quality. The findings indicate that private equity-backed firms have higher levels of earnings management in the pre-financing years than non-backed ones, suggesting that entrepreneurs use earnings to attract investors. Also, private equity-backed firms have a higher tendency to report losses in good time compared to non-private equity-backed equivalents from the private equity financing year onwards. The results of Beuselinck et al. show that firms looking for private equity voluntarily disclose more information than legally required to signal their quality to outsiders.

It is a long time before private equity investors get their money back. Those investors who have been in the industry for a long time know that the short repayment periods for funds created in the second half of the 1990s will not come again soon. In Chapter 4, Kaserer and Diller bring new insights into the performance measures of equity funds, whose factors impact on these returns, and further, to what extent it might be possible to predict such returns. In particular, their objective is to test the 'money-chasing deals' phenomenon, that is, the effect of cash inflows into private equity funds on an individual fund performance. Their perspective is completed with the analysis of the impact of fund managers' skills on performance. The results show that a fund formed in periods of high absolute inflows (originated by economic prospects) and low relative inflows (signal of low intensity of deal competition) obtains relatively high returns compared to funds founded in years with low absolute inflows (hence no extraordinary economic perspectives) and high relative inflows directed to a fund (signal of high competition for deals) obtain low returns.

Prior to testing the money-chasing deals phenomenon, the authors propose a new way to avoid the shortcomings of the usual internal rate of return (IRR) measure: the excess IRR, the price market on earnings (PME) and the undiscounted payback period methods. They also suggest adjusting returns for management fees and conclude that the PME is the most adequate method. Finally, sustaining the evidence proposed by Barnes and Menzies (Chapter 1), the authors suggest that funds tend to maintain their status as high or low performers. Hence, the common strategy among LP analysts is reinvesting in funds with which they had good experiences proofs positive.

Informal investors, or 'business angels', complete the spectrum of external equity financing available for new and young ventures (called the 'early-stage market'). These investors do not make the headlines because they invest their own money directly and hence do not need to market their activity, or establish any reputation in the market; moreover, often they wish to keep their investment activities unknown.

An ongoing concern is the relatively lower development of the European informal market as compared to that in the US. In Chapter 5, Roure et al. suggest that one of the reasons for the scarcity of business angels in the EU landscape is the lack of individuals with specific investment expertise. The authors underline that there are many potential investors, all with relevant industry, sector knowledge or entrepreneurial experience, often lacking the necessary capabilities to face investing in new, innovative and often technology-based business.

Roure et al. identify significant differences between potential (those who have not yet closed the first deal) and active investors. While both types, 'virgin' and active angels, have similar wealth profiles and investment preferences (in terms of amount, sector or stage), the proportion of business owners and entrepreneurs is notably higher among active angels. According to the authors there are important benefits for business schools in training potential investors in the management of the entire investment process. The authors also explore the benefits for active and virgin angels from joining a business angel academy. In particular, academies provide a first starting point to help angels to identify and evaluate investment proposals. Those investors that are already active find it an excellent place to exchange experience with other active angels and to improve certain aspects of investment management.

2.2   Part II: The Entrepreneur's Perspective on the Role of Private Equity

This middle part of the book includes four chapters that cover the ways in which entrepreneurs and new venture managers approach the venture capital acquisition process and the impact of correctly managing the relationship with investors on performance. First, we recall the direct link between venture capital and growth. A potential source of growth for companies is the development of international activities. Venture capitalists can support companies along this process by providing their experience and networks. In an increasingly pan-European venture capital market, investors find an increasing facility to move cross-border. Many decide to establish a foreign representative office, a subsidiary office or, on the contrary, manage investments from their home country.

Using a novel theoretical approach, the means–end chain from marketing disciplines, Morandin et al. (Chapter 6) investigate the motivations of entrepreneurs to engage in a search for venture capital. Their model places motives not so much in reference to internal stimuli *per se*, but in terms of achieving goals. In their study, they present three broad categories of motives to use venture capital. One category is linked to market and business dimensions, the second contains firm variables while the third is linked to the entrepreneur *per se*, with aspects reflecting personal goals and one's family. Morandin et al. recognize that an important drawback of their research is the thin line between the first and the second categories. Their chapter shows that the main motivations for demanding venture capital are firm growth, competitiveness and managerial competence, respectively. However, these motives are not stand-alone elements; on the contrary, there are significant links between them. For instance, growth and competitiveness are difficult to disentangle. It is important to note that in their study the authors do not propose up-front categories of motivations to entrepreneurs surveyed and interviewed, rather, entrepreneurs were asked to list their personal reasons for choosing a goal, the importance of this goal and to explain why such a goal was important.

From the contribution by Hogan and Hutson (Chapter 7) we learn that the use of venture capital seems to be related to certain traits of the lead founder, the funding team, product lead times, start-up costs and willingness to relinquish control. Research on the inclination of management teams to use venture capital has led to surprising results. The authors believe that entrepreneurs with previous start-up experience do not use more venture capital than entrepreneurs with no prior start-up experience. These findings are inconsistent with the traditional wisdom suggesting that previous experience is critical to attract venture capital.

For Hogan and Hutson, clearly, the factors for granting venture capital are not the same factors as for demanding it. Related to the background of founders and the use of venture capital, the authors find mixed evidence, there is no relation between education beyond degree level and venture capital backing. However, there seems to be a positive relationship between such backing and degree-level qualification. A further finding in relation to the founding team concerns its size, which seems to bear no implications for demanding venture capital. Hogan and Hutson claim that the lead time does not seem to influence entrepreneurs' attraction towards venture capital. Finally, the authors find a positive and strong relationship between venture founders' willingness to relinquish control and venture backing. The results show that many experienced teams eschew venture capitalists. They conclude that many new technology-based firms do not make themselves available for venture capital funding.

In Chapter 8, Mäkelä and Maula explore the role of foreign-based VCs in supporting the internationalization of new software ventures. Hence their study claims an active role for the venture itself to look for investors that might grant them relationships with other agents in an unknown environment for them and to select the best-positioned investor to contribute to their internationalization plans. For Mäkelä and Maula, the presence of foreign investors is likely to lead to a process in which the investee firm becomes more similar to companies in the geographic areas where the investors have a presence. This chapter outlines how the benefits of cross-border investors are realized: increasing venture legitimacy by providing endorsement, providing knowledge of the business and legal environment, and bringing international social capital. The authors suggest that cross-border venture capital investors will decrease the liability of foreignness.

The authors do not neglect negative costs associated with the participation of cross-border VCs, the most important being the push to internationalize to 'incorrect' markets, that is, to markets not optimal for the growth of the venture, which might be the case of a market where the investor is based or present. It is very important that the new venture chooses investors located in markets central to their internationalization strategy; that is, investors must ensure target market fit, and be willing and able to help ventures to expand there. They claim that if this market fit does not exist, the presence of cross-border venture capital might bring increased costs or incorrect internationalization. They add that entrepreneurs should look for investors able to provide endorsement, international social capital, and foreign organizing knowledge.

Part II ends by recalling some of the elements discussed with regard to performance measurement by venture capitalists developed previously by Kaserer and Diller (Chapter 4). Here the researchers introduce an element of subjectivity in measuring the performance achieved. In Chapter 9, De Clercq et al. approach the issue from a crucial angle for entrepreneurs and managers. The authors demonstrate that higher levels of trust, social interaction and goal congruence in the relationship between the investor and the investee company result in higher perceived performance. Also the same effect emanates from a high commitment, defined as the intensity of the relationship between both parties, on the part of the VCs. The authors found that the existence of a relationship in the above terms helps the VCs understand the operations and needs of the company and positively colours perceptions of performance. The reverse argument is more straightforward, if the relationship with the investee is bad, poor performance will look worse to VCs; if the relationship is good, VCs might give poor performers the benefit of the doubt and judge good performers even better. Nevertheless De Clercq et al. do not claim that VCs assess company performance based on whether they 'like' the company or not. On the contrary, they identify learning effects on discerning actual performance, which ultimately dominate their judgement. Finally, the authors advise entrepreneurs seeking to maximize their benefit from the venture capital provider to be willing to build strong interpersonal relationships with representatives of the venture capital firm. In a broader sense, their findings suggest that companies may increase their reputation in the venture capital community by engaging in open communication with their investors.

2.3   Part III: Private Equity and the Role of Public Policy in Europe

For the third part of this book we have reserved four chapters that explore two key issues that have received extensive attention from our policy makers:

spin-out companies and the equity gap. Chapters 10 and 11 cover the problematic regarding the creation and growth of companies transferring university-developed technology to the market, and Chapter 12 revises the accepted wisdom on the equity gap. The concluding chapter brings both issues together and places them in a European context.

In Chapter 10, Wright and Lockett deepen the insights advanced in the contribution of Harrison and Leitch, including the perspectives of the parties involved in spin-out development investors and technology transfer offices (TTOs). The authors conceptualize the problems faced by entrepreneurs in a system of critical junctures: opportunity recognition, entrepreneurial commitment, credibility and sustainability. The study proposes that spin-outs secure a strong partnership base with different kinds of agents in their environment, attract a champion committed to the entrepreneurial development (whether this champion is initially internal or external to the venture), and demonstrate the viability of their business proposal, for instance in terms of intellectual property protection or proof of concept. To earmark sustainability, the spin-out needs accessing and integrating resources and capabilities. Due to from the above-mentioned critical junctures that spin-outs must overcome, investors look carefully for certain assets within the investment proposals they receive.

Wright and Lockett highlight the perceived difference in the risk/return relationship of investors between spin-outs and other technology ventures and propose that in particular, those investors less prone to spin-out investment should demand a relevant size of the potential market, joint ownership of intellectual property rights (IPRs) with a university, existence of a prototype, and 'identifiability' of key decision makers or perspectives for the development of a sophisticated product or service. Last but not least, the quality and composition of the management team is an essential part of the investment decision when screening proposals. The authors acknowledge that not a few efforts have been dedicated to highlighting the importance of investment readiness of business proposals, especially important in the case of early investment in general and spin-outs in particular. The authors put forward a criterion that all investors have in mind, whether they have a higher or lower propensity towards spin-out investment, that is, the time to realize their investment through an exit, or at least the stage when the venture can attract other co-investors to share the risk and provide follow-on finance. In fact the authors remind us that too often spin-out ventures cannot promise/deliver the speed of development that would attract VCs.

Public policy makers, whether at regional, national or European level have recognized the difficulties of new and young ventures to attract finance. This inefficiency of the market to provide finance, between the stage where entrepreneurs' and their family wealth is sufficient to fund the business and the stage when venture capital funds are broadly interested in investing, is referred to as the 'equity gap'.

In Chapter 11, Harrison and Leitch hint at the contribution that spin-out companies make to the development of the regions where they are located. The findings of their study lead them to think that many university spin-outs are more like technology lifestyle ventures rather than entrepreneurial businesses. Hence, also from the university point of view spin-outs are not likely to be a major source of income as compared to licensing or other technology transfer activities.

The authors point out the specific difficulties of spin-outs, for instance when trying to channel the evolution of an initial idea into a non-commercial environment and becoming established as competitive rent-generating firms. The authors find that one of the origins of the lack of growth orientation among university spin-outs is related to the presence of 'academic' entrepreneurs, less ambitious than classic entrepreneurs, and perhaps also less aware of their business's innovation and development needs. For Harrison and Leitch, these academic entrepreneurs often conceive their business opportunity in terms of a strong technological advance, rather than on the consideration of the market need for such a product. The research carried out suggests that company spin-outs are based on the exploitation of very small portfolios of protectable intellectual property (IP).

With regard to the role played by the universities, the chapter indicates that spin-outs value in particular university support for their entrepreneurial efforts to exploit technology, clarifying the legal IP position and providing pre-company formation business advice. Indeed, the authors maintain that there is room for improvement within universities regarding identification and exploitation of market opportunity for the technology in different ways and in providing alternative career options.

In Chapter 12, Murray and Dimov investigate the factors that influence early-stage investment and the factors that contribute to a more intensive activity within the early-stage market. Contrary to the belief that it is the smaller venture capital funds that invest in the earlier stages, the authors suggest that older and larger funds seem to be taking the initiative in this segment of the market. In this line, their findings might throw some doubts on the public policy towards venture capital in place in most European countries and at EU level. The chapter reminds us that current policies place smaller and technology-oriented funds at the core of policy instruments and this might not deliver the sought benefits.

Murray and Dimov provide evidence of the existence of a minimum and a maximum scale efficiency in making seed investments. Hence, up to a certain portfolio size, the larger a fund is the more prone it would be to invest in the early stage. Once the portfolio exceeds that maximum activity, its investments in the seed stage will decrease. On the contrary, the relationship between the total amounts invested by the fund suggests a minimum size to start considering seed investments. Nevertheless, the authors claim that the characteristics of the fund *per se* are not sufficient to explain early-stage activity.

Other elements, such as the education and industry experience of the top management team members, influence this propensity. Executives with a background in finance tend to be more reluctant to invest in the earlier stage, probably due to their conservative objective, more related to minimizing losses, or bankruptcies, than to maximizing success. Further, the authors point out that previous experience is critical not only as to how investments are perceived or chosen, but also regarding their management, pointing to a highly subjective investment process within the venture capital industry.

Finally, the predispositions of an individual investor or an investment analyst are important to understand which proposals make it through the first cut in the screening selection process within a VC fund. These individual characteristics are difficult for entrepreneurs approaching venture capital funds, making passing the first selection cut highly dependent on the proposal reaching the right hands.

The concluding chapter by Schamp (Chapter 13) deals with the European challenge formulated by the Lisbon European Council of 2000, setting the strategic goal for the European Union to become the most competitive and dynamic knowledge-based economy in the world by 2010. Europe's researchers are among the world's leaders in many areas of technological research and development but much of their exploitable work never reaches the marketplace. Improving the commercialization rate of inventions and research-based innovation is one way for Europe to raise its competitive performance. Taking an innovation from the laboratory to the point at which private commercial investors are willing to fund it as a start-up requires a variety of inputs that in many cases can be supplied with a relatively modest amount of finance. The private sector, acting alone, tends – for sound economic reasons – to produce a rate of throughput that is suboptimal from the public policy viewpoint. Responses to the problem across and outside Europe have taken a wide variety of financial, institutional and organizational approaches. Many programmes have been initiated over the past five years.

While presenting some of the main outcomes and conclusions of the PAXIS and Gate2Growth initiatives Schamp also discusses the European agenda for stimulating academic entrepreneurship, creating a more entrepreneurial culture at European universities and research centres, leading to more effective technology transfer and more successful spin-out programmes and for bridging the finance gap.

In general, there is a long way to go in order to maximize benefits from university and public research through the creation of spin-outs. Therefore it is necessary to increase efforts to make technology transfer offices more professional. These, before all other parties concerned, should inform academic entrepreneurs and tech start-ups of the differences between potential investment channels and the impact of this on their venture and on how to approach VCs. There is a strong need to revise public policy with regard to venture capital, including to refocus on small funds and increase efforts with regard to the business angel community.

PART I

The Financial Community's Perspective on the Role of Private Equity

1. Investment in venture capital funds in Europe

Simon Barnes and Vanessa Menzies*

---

1. INTRODUCTION

The creation of entrepreneurial new ventures is critically dependent on a plentiful supply of venture capital (VC) finance within the economy. Entrepreneurs need venture capital finance to grow their businesses and, likewise, venture capitalists (VCs) need entrepreneurs to generate a return. The delicate mating dance between the two sides of this capital equation has, for many years, been the focus of research into the venture capital industry. Indeed, how VCs select the ventures they back has been mapped in detail to show that there are five or six sequential steps to any venture capital decision process. These steps include deal origination, screening, evaluation, structuring and post-investment activities (for example, Tyebjee and Bruno, 1984). A great deal of research has also highlighted the range of selection criteria employed at each stage of the process such as the size of the investment, the technology or product, the industry-sector geographic location and investment stage.

As illustrated in Figure 1.1, however, VCs are not the ultimate providers of capital for entrepreneurial ventures; they do not sit at the beginning of the capital supply chain. VCs are, instead, hands-on intermediaries who provide an interface between the providers of capital (the investors in their fund, for example, pension funds, investment trusts, banks or wealthy clients) and the entrepreneurs who utilize such capital to create successful businesses. VCs screen, monitor, advise and assist in investments; they manage information asymmetry and decrease agency costs, providing their investors with access to investment opportunities that they would not normally be equipped to undertake.

While the venture capital decision-making process has been explored in detail, there is less research examining the decision processes and criteria of investors in VC funds (generally referred to as limited partners or LPs). In other words we know a lot about how VCs choose entrepreneurs but very little about how VCs themselves are selected by their limited partners one step further back in the capital supply chain. For example, do LPs identify

3

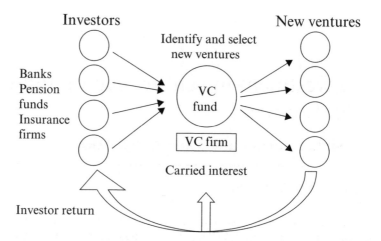

Note: VC firms raise funds (often structured as limited partnerships) from investors (the LPs) such as banks, pension funds and insurance companies to invest in new ventures such as start-ups and management buy-outs. The VC selects and monitors investments in new ventures and distributes returns to investors in shares or cash, with the VC receiving a proportion of the gain as 'carried interest'. Most research has focused on the relationship between the venture capital firm and the new venture. This chapter moves a step further back in the capital supply chain and examines the relationship between LPs and VCs in detail.

Figure 1.1   The role of the venture capitalist

and invest in VCs on an *ad hoc* basis or do they conduct structured searches and rigorous evaluation procedures?

Understanding how and why limited partners select VC funds is crucial to understanding the supply of venture capital finance and hence the creation of entrepreneurial ventures. This research is intended to be useful to VCs raising funds and to entrepreneurs and LPs in understanding further the dynamics of the venture capital cycle.

2.   THE EFFECTS OF REPUTATION

At the macroeconomic level, research has examined the overall supply and demand for venture capital finance and its impact on venture capital fundraising. Several studies have examined the competitive environment within which VCs operate and have highlighted the increasing competition between VCs to raise funds from investors. Gompers and Lerner (1999a) suggested that the ability of VCs to attract investment is related to previous fund performance and 'reputation', measured as venture capital firm age and fund size. Other authors have shown that the size of a VC fund is often a function of past success and reputation. The notion of venture capital reputation has been explored further by Van Osnabrugge and Robinson (2001) who stated that venture capital reputation is the aggregate culmination of many small procedures, conduct and performance levels which the venture capital firm maintains. They suggest that VCs who are dependent on raising external capital behave more diligently and play a greater monitoring role than 'captive' VCs, employed by large financial institutions, in order to signal their investment skills to LPs and maximize their chances of raising subsequent funds.

Previous research has suggested, therefore, that a VC's ability to raise funds is related to multiple measures of their reputation and that VCs signal such reputation to potential LPs. The aim of our research, therefore, was to explore the decision processes and criteria utilized by LPs in Europe. In particular, we have examined LPs' perceptions of venture capital 'reputation' and how decisions are operationalized.

3. RESULTS

Our results represent the findings of 40 hours of interviews with senior management at 21 LPs throughout Europe. The LPs we spoke to managed between €150 million and €5000 million and represented a mix of pension funds, insurance companies, banks and other professional organizations investing in VC funds as well as other 'asset classes' such as public stocks, property, bonds and money markets.

We found that LPs utilize a structured process when originating and selecting venture capital firms in which to invest. In general, they do not invest *ad hoc* in venture capital firms that approach them or when the opportunity arises. LPs follow clear procedures for managing the annual allocation of capital to VCs as an asset class, often seeking formal budget approval from an investment board. The results summarized in Figure 1.2, suggest that the processes for the selection of VC funds can be divided into two levels, (i) the overall budget allocation of capital to venture capital versus public stocks or other asset classes and (ii) the selection of individual VC funds in which to invest the allocated capital.

A large proportion of LPs also utilize a stage we have referred to as 'screening II' in which investors hold meetings with VCs, often to build relationships for future investments into the fund. A majority of LPs build consensus early in the selection process by utilizing a gate-keeping stage we have referred to as 'ratification'.

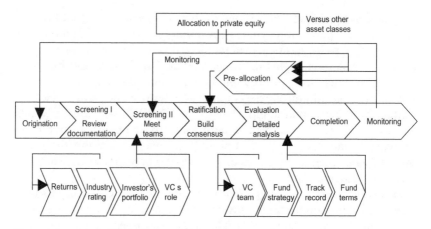

Note: LPs originate VC fund opportunities through a variety of sources and progress funds to a screening stage where documentation is reviewed and criteria including historical returns, industry ratings within, the LP's portfolio diversification strategy, and notably whether the venture capital is 'hands on' or not.

Figure 1.2   Processes utilized by LPs for investment in VC funds

Ratification involves a 'sanity check' with the senior managers within the LP and appears to serve the purpose of minimizing the opportunity cost of evaluating VC funds that the LP rejects at later stages. Evaluation consists of detailed analysis of numerous criteria, the most important of which are the VC's team, the strategy for investing the VC fund, the track record of previous VC funds (including whether the team delivered the original strategy) and finally fund investment terms. The overall allocation to VCs as an 'asset class' sets the budget for investing in VC funds. We observed that LPs will pre-allocate capital to VC funds that they have backed previously or VC funds they may have tracked via meetings conducted at the screening II stage. This emphasizes the difficulty faced by new venture capital firms of raising a first fund. If a portion of investors' annual capital allocation to private equity is pre-allocated to existing funds, then the barriers to entry for raising a new fund are significant.

3.1   Sources of Capital Influence the Decision Process

It became clear early in the interview process that just as VCs may be classified based on their sources of capital, whether internal or external to the firm (Van Osnabrugge and Robinson, 2001), LPs in our sample also exhibited a variety of sources of capital.

Balance sheet investors

Balance sheet investors are investment teams that operate within large financial institutions and invest their parent organization's capital, that is, from the balance sheet of the institution. For the most part, investment teams operate as distinct units with dedicated in-house fund managers for investments in venture capital, similar to the 'captive' VCs described by Van Osnabrugge and Robinson (2001).

Hybrid investors

Hybrid investors are investment teams that operate within large financial institutions and invest from the balance sheet of their parent institution *and* on behalf of third party external investors, that is, they manage external capital as well as that of the parent.

Specialist investors

Specialist investors manage third party capital only, and hence are entirely dependent on raising external capital to survive.

Gatekeepers

Gatekeepers are professionals who advise LPs on investment in VC funds for a fee, but do not manage the capital that is invested. They have been described by previous authors and appear to play a key role in structuring investment vehicles specifically to their clients' individual requirements.

Our research showed that specialist investors have, in general, been investing in VC funds for longer periods of time than hybrid investors, who in turn have been investing longer than balance sheet investors. There are two explanations for this observation: either investing from the balance sheet is a recent phenomenon, or alternatively, as investment business units mature they evolve to raise external capital. When respondents were questioned about this point, they stated that as investment teams become more experienced and establish a reputation, they are able to attract external capital. Respondents associated the raising of external capital with greater decision-making power and the perception of greater remuneration packages for the investment teams. This suggests that investment teams themselves are the driving force for such transitions, implying that they follow an evolutionary pathway, illustrated in Figure 1.3, towards the creation of specialist, and ultimately independent investment firms as they gain experience and track record in the sector.

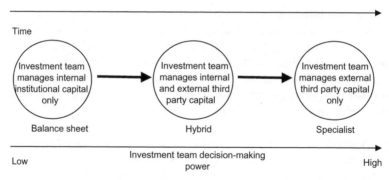

Figure 1.3   The evolution of LPs

3.2   Allocation to Venture Capital and Team Structure

For the majority of investors in our sample the decision to invest in VC funds for the first time had been taken at least two years prior to the date of this study. We focused, therefore, on the processes by which capital is allocated to the venture capital sector on an ongoing basis. The study highlighted that differences in an LP's own source of capital are indeed associated with different processes and criteria for the annual budget allocation to venture capital.

For balance sheet investors, the budget allocation to venture capital is normally built around a two-tier structure with operational investment teams reporting to an investment board that controls strategy. The board relies heavily on recommendations from the investment team and decides the overall allocation to venture capital based on an annual business plan. LPs highlighted several drawbacks within this structure from the perspective of the investment team. As one respondent stated, the board occasionally required the investment team to 'plug a profit gap on the institutions' P&L' by realizing an investment at a time felt by the investment team to be suboptimal. This is consistent with the suggestions of Van Osnabrugge and Robinson (2001) that managers within such institutions have 3–4-year job horizons and, therefore, may choose to focus on short-term gains to the detriment of long-term potential. Finally, these units, albeit distinct, do not for the most part possess a separate profit and loss (P&L) and do not receive management fees from their parent institution. Several respondents highlighted this as a de-motivating factor for the investment team.

Hybrid investors employed a similar capital allocation strategy, with an annual strategic review by the board determining the allocation to, and overall strategy of, the institution to investing in venture capital. This also included commitments by the institution to any new funds being raised by the investment teams that would contain external capital.

This contrasts with specialist investors, for whom the allocation of capital is driven by the senior management within the firm and is largely dependent upon the fund-raising climate. The funding cycle implies that at any one time LPs might be raising capital while simultaneously investing capital raised previously. Similar to the VCs they back, the LPs in general raise capital in 2–3-year cycles. It is tempting to speculate that positive fund-raising climates may give rise to opportunistic attempts by LPs to raise additional capital similar to that displayed by venture capital firms or to 'grandstand' in order to signal their reputation to potential investors in their own funds (Gompers and Lerner, 1999b).

3.3 Selection Philosophy: Objective versus Subjective

The underlying principles for the selection of VC funds can be grouped broadly into objective and subjective criteria. At one extreme we were able to identify LPs who are primarily *objective* in their investment philosophy. These LPs are methodical and process driven, rely heavily on benchmarking of VC funds and ensure that minimum quantifiable performance hurdles are met. VCs are often graded using a matrix system, allocating weighted scores to required criteria. At the other extreme, we were also able to identify investors who are more *subjective* in their approach, and who view the investment process as more qualitative. Such investors tend to have longer investing track records than those who take a more objective approach, and like more experienced VCs relied more on intuition and experience.

3.4 The Processes and Criteria Utilized in the Selection of VC Funds

Our model for investment in VC funds (shown in Figure 1.2) is divided into two levels of decision-making – a budget allocation process for venture capital as an asset class followed by a decision process for investing in individual VC funds.

LPs adopt a structured process through which VC funds are identified and subjected to increasing levels of scrutiny. We termed these stages 'origination', 'screening' and 'evaluation' following the terminology of authors studying VC processes.

3.5 Screening

As opposed to the existing venture capital literature, 'screening' in this instance comprises a number of specific, and separate activities that warrant designation as sub-stages of the screening activity. We have defined these screening stages as 'screening I' in which the fund document- ation is vetted; 'screening II' in which investors conducted introductory meetings with VCs but did not embark upon detailed assessment; and 'ratification' in which the investment team agrees formally to proceed to a more costly and laborious evaluation stage in which detailed due diligence is carried out.

Screening II (in other words meeting with venture capital teams as a matter of routine) is used by established investors to identify a core group of VCs whose performance they track, irrespective of whether they are current investors in the VCs' funds. This acts as a source of market intelli- gence and potential future opportunities to invest. In other words, LPs begin to form opinions and make decisions regarding VCs well before VCs begin the fund-raising process, and may pre-allocate capital to those VCs they have targeted for investment.

The selection criteria at the screening stage that investors cited most often were: (i) magnitude and consistency of historic returns of previous funds; (ii) rating of the VCs' previous returns as 'top quartile' by specialist databases such as Venture Economics; (iii) the LP's diversification strategy; and (iv) the perception of the VC as 'hands on' and 'adding value' to the portfolio companies in which they invest.

The last point is somewhat surprising and demonstrates that investors do not rely on historical return as an indicator of future performance. Whether VCs really do add value to the ventures they back is up for debate, but it appears that LPs perceive this as an important screening criterion for investing. This suggests that VCs should act as 'hands-on' investors to maximize their chances of raising capital. Indeed, one LP in our survey commented that for VCs to justify the annual management fee they command, 'they have to demonstrate that they can make more money than we would'. Our data support the view, therefore, that VCs who remain passive in their approach to monitoring investments will find it increasingly difficult to raise future capital from investors.

Following screening of investment opportunities either via the fund documentation, published data or meetings with the VCs, the majority of investors in our sample employed a *ratification* stage at which consensus was reached to proceed to evaluation of the opportunity. Ratification consisted of either a formal investment review or a discussion within the team to build consensus at an early stage in the selection process. These findings suggest that consensus building, either the formal endorsement of fellow team members or an investment committee, is seen as a prior- ity by investment teams at early stages of the venture capital selection process.

3.6 Evaluation

Our results showed that the evaluation stage prioritized four key criteria.

The team
LPs evaluate the mix and balance of relevant experience and the stability and homogeneity of the team. Notably, respondents in our sample group did not highlight individual qualifications as a priority but were more concerned with the extent to which the existing team had worked together rather than the performance of one or two key individuals, suggesting a focus on consistency and continuity within the team rather than dependence on individuals. LPs also highlighted work allocation and incentivization within the team, supporting previous findings that incentivization of younger VCs within the team is seen as an important motivating factor to drive their performance (Gompers and Lerner, 1999a); in other words, investors were not attracted to venture capital firms where the wealthiest managing partners took 'the lion's share' of carried interest in new funds but were less active operationally. LPs also focused on the VC's reputation among entrepreneurs they have backed and existing investors in their funds.

Track record
Whereas VCs investing in a new venture rarely have the opportunity to assess the entrepreneur's performance in similar previous ventures, investors in VC funds are often able to assess, quantitatively, the performance of previous funds the venture capital firm has managed. LPs in our sample looked at a range of quantitative measures of historical fund performance including net internal rate of return (IRR), the return multiple, and percentage of investments realized versus unrealized over the life of the fund. A key issue was whether significant gains on investments could be assigned to 'luck', that is, isolated exit events at unpredictable market peaks, versus the team genuinely and consistently adding value to investments. LPs in our sample focused on consistency of performance by examining holding periods for investments and subsequent return multiples rather than IRRs which may be impacted by short-term gains and grandstanding.

Strategy
The key issue addressed by LPs appeared to be whether the venture capital had executed the strategy proposed in previous funds and whether the same strategy would be successful again. Consistency appeared to be the key question for the majority of investors, specifically whether previous funds had been invested according to plan. The majority of investors in our

survey approached investors in the VC's previous funds to assess whether previous strategies had been delivered.

Fund terms and conditions

One LP summarized the general attitude towards the terms and conditions of the fund by stating 'what is the point of negotiating good terms on the investment if the management teams are no good and the fund loses money – you just have good terms on nothing'. LPs stated that investment agreements adhere to standard market terms, which most claimed to be familiar with, and perceive the investment agreement as being of little consequence in their decisions. Such standardization of agreements appeared to have encouraged a number of LPs in our sample to nurture informal relationships with VCs outside the contractual relationship of the investment agreement. For example, it is rare for an investor to secure a contractual right to co-invest with the venture capital in selected new ventures but they perceive that a close non-contractual relationship provides a 'favoured status' for access to potential deals.

4.2   CONCLUSION AND IMPLICATIONS

Limited partners in VC funds follow a procedure for selecting VCs similar to the processes used by VCs themselves in selecting new ventures, and which have been studied in detail by previous authors. We found that like the VC funds in which they invest, LPs follow a sequence of deal origination, screening, evaluation and finally completion with a range of criteria being applied at each decision point prior to completion of the investment agreement.

There are, however, important differences to the processes reported for VCs. Perhaps most notable is the observation that investors build consensus within the investment team very early in the selection process, via a stage we have referred to as ratification. Ratification represents a formal decision to proceed, either via a presentation to an investment committee or a meeting within the investment team. It is not surprising that investment decisions are made via consensus building, but that consensus building occurs so early in the process indicates that investors place a heavy emphasis on gaining the support of their colleagues before progressing. The opportunity costs for progressing venture capital firms to later evaluation stages are presumably high, with limited resources within the investment team being diverted away from more promising opportunities. It is likely that investment institutions perceive these opportunity costs and follow procedures to minimize them, perhaps utilizing the input of senior team members or an investment committee to guide less experienced investment managers away from evaluating unlikely deals.

Our research supports the view that LPs examine broad, and often intangible, indicators of venture capital reputation in an attempt to assess future performance. LPs appear to look beyond the financial performance of previous funds and, perhaps appreciating that past success does not reflect future potential, examine other aspects of venture capital reputation in an attempt to assess potential future performance. They approach entrepreneurs, other VCs and other investors to assess venture capital reputation from different viewpoints, leading us to conclude that entrepreneurs in fact play a role in the investor–venture capital relationship. LPs rate the perception of VCs as 'hands on' as an important screening criterion necessary even to progress a VC to the evaluation stage of the selection process. That VCs' reputation as 'hands on' is a priority for LPs indicates that LPs appear to regard the VCs whom they back as value-adding intermediaries who must earn their relatively large management fees by providing a one-stop shop for entrepreneurs to maximize the value of the LP's investment.

The uncertainty of evaluating which VCs to invest in may explain why LPs appear to track, and then back, a core group of VCs with whom they develop long-term relationships. Respondents in our survey relied heavily on continued investments in VCs they have backed previously, pre-allocating capital from their venture capital budget in anticipation of future fund-raising activities of their favourite VCs. This indicates that a VC's fate may be sealed before he/she walks through the LP's door. If they are among the core group of favoured VCs they may find themselves in the fortunate position of fast tracking through the selection process (see Figure 1.2). This finding has highlighted an important issue: investors utilize different processes and criteria for VCs they have backed previously compared to VCs they have not invested in before. Thus our model for investment into VC funds incorporates pre-allocation to favoured VCs with whom a relationship exists.

This finding illustrates the difficulties faced by new venture capital firms in breaking into a fund-raising market where decisions to invest may have been made, at least in part, even before VCs approach investors. The pre-allocation of capital to tried and tested VCs raises significant barriers to entry to new VCs but also highlights an issue for investors. By investing further capital in VCs they have already backed, investors expose themselves to diversification risk – placing their faith in a limited number of VCs. Just as VCs may overlook a fundamentally flawed opportunity due to the reputation of a previously successful entrepreneur, LPs may place too much faith in the reputation and relationship they have built with previously successful VCs. In addition, VCs who raise a new fund while simultaneously investing in a previous fund are able to spend proportionately less time investing in the new fund and may even create conflicts of interest between successive funds through their decisions on where to focus their time and efforts.

A notable finding in our study is that LPs place a heavy emphasis on the development of a strong informal relationship with VCs outside the formal terms of the investment agreement. The relationship is perceived as an important means of accessing the best VC funds in which to invest and perhaps making direct co-investments in new ventures.

Our chapter highlights that although the formal investment agreement is a necessity, the informal relationship is a key mechanism for stabilizing the investor–venture capital relationship throughout the cycle of shifting supply and demand, that is, both parties appear to remain committed to each other beyond the formal terms of their agreement. Recent research has shown that entrepreneurs' social competence (such as their accuracy in perceiving others) is positively related to their financial success. Similarly, it is tempting to speculate that the social competence of both LP and VC in perceiving each other may be an important component of a long and successful financial relationship.

Our research has attempted to explore the criteria and processes utilized by professional investors in VC funds. Our findings are summarized in Figure 1.2 as a model for the decision-making processes and criteria of investors in VC funds (LPs). We have emphasized the role of the VC as a financial intermediary, subject to the pressures of raising funds in order to ensure their continued ability to invest in new ventures. By exploring the processes and criteria employed by investors, it is hoped that this chapter will provide useful findings for venture capital investors in establishing benchmark criteria and processes, and for new venture capital firms attempting to negotiate the difficulties of raising funds.

For VCs the delicate art of courting investment from Europe's leading investors must begin early, and perhaps be maintained through a series of funds before investors will commit. This may not be a surprise for anyone with experience of the venture capital fundraising cycle but there are subtleties to the conclusion that warrant further explanation. We observed that many LPs *pre-allocate* capital to venture capital firms they have backed previously in anticipation of repeat fundraisings. For new VCs raising their first fund, this raises the bar even higher than was previously thought in securing commitment from LPs.

From the perspective of LPs, such a recurring commitment to tried-and-tested VCs may enable them to place a greater amount of capital with minimal effort, and perhaps at a perceived lower risk. There is a note of caution for LPs, however, in that repeated commitment to the same group of trusted VCs creates a diversification risk. LPs should think carefully about their investment strategy and broaden their perspective on selecting new funds.

This chapter serves as an exploratory study of decision making upstream from the VC–entrepreneur relationship and extends our understanding of the interactions between LP and VC, and hence the overall flow of capital into new ventures. It has become clear through the course of this study that the standardization of limited partnership agreements has resulted in LPs and VCs placing great emphasis on informal relationships as a means of cementing long-term commitment to each other.

NOTE

* The authors wish to thank Professor Sue Birley and Dr Nicos Nicolau of Imperial College (London, UK), for constructive comments during the preparation of this chapter.

REFERENCES

Gompers, P.A. and Lerner, J. (1999a), 'What drives venture capital fundraising?', *Brookings Papers on Economic Activity*, July, 149–92.
Gompers, P.A. and Lerner, J. (1999b), *The Venture Capital Cycle*, Cambridge, MA: MIT Press.
Tyebjee, T.T. and Bruno, A.V. (1984), 'A model of venture capitalist investment activity', *Management Science*, **30**, 1051–66.
Van Osnabrugge, M. and Robinson, R.J. (2001), 'The influence of a venture capitalist's source of funds', *Venture Capital*, **3**, 25–39.

2. An analysis of the selection behaviour of early-stage high-tech investors in Europe

Bart Clarysse, Mirjam Knockaert, Andy Lockett and Caroline Van Eeckhout

1. INTRODUCTION

Even though research into decision criteria has been a major topic over the past two decades, most studies have been undertaken with US-based venture capitalists (VCs), and have focused on the venture capital industry as a whole. Several researchers have, however, indicated that high-tech investing is different (for example, Lockett et al., 2002) from non-tech investing and that early-stage investing is different from late-stage investing. This chapter focuses on how the specific group of early-stage high-tech venture capitalists make their investment decisions.

First, we look at how these early-stage high-tech investors select their investments, and which selection criteria matter. Second, we look at what determines differences in selection behaviour. This research, using a novel methodology, is carried out in seven selected high-tech regions in Europe that have a high venture capital presence.

Previous research has identified a number of important criteria on which VC firms base their decision to invest. Some researchers found that the ability of the entrepreneurs (such as management skills and management team) mattered most (Tyebjee and Bruno, 1984; MacMillan et al., 1985, 1987; Shepherd and Zacharakis, 1998). Some found the market environment of the new venture to be the most determining selection criterion for VCs (Hisrich and Jankowitz, 1990; Muzyka et al., 1996). Others found the financial criteria, exit opportunities and product/service characteristics to be the most important selection criteria (MacMillan et al., 1987).

Even though these previous studies have revealed interesting and useful insights, they were often criticized for using simple methodologies for assessing the evaluation criteria. For instance, they asked investment managers why they invested in certain proposals (called *post hoc* methodology), which is problematic given that individuals have limited capacity to recall what has happened, or could bias results. A second stream of researchers used real-time methods during which VCs had to think aloud, and from which the hierarchy of selection criteria was derived. This method is criticized as it can give rise to subjectivity during interpretation.

Therefore, in this research on selection behaviour of early-stage high-tech investors, we use a quite novel methodology: conjoint analysis. Using this methodology, 68 early-stage high-tech investors in seven European high-tech regions were interviewed in the course of 2003. In what follows, we first provide more information on the high-tech regions included in this research and the methodology used. Second, we provide an overview of the most important findings of this research, indicating what criteria early-stage high-tech investors base their investment decision on, and indicating what factors determine this investment behaviour. Finally, we provide a conclusion and implications for practitioners.

2. SAMPLE AND METHODOLOGY

First, we discuss the sample of early-stage high-tech investors. Second, we provide an overview of the methodology used.

Given that no complete database of early-stage high-tech investors in the selected regions was available, a dataset was constructed using several sources.

We used the directory of the European Venture Capital Association (EVCA) as a starting point. The EVCA runs conferences in the domain of venture capital, provides training to venture capital professionals and carries out research among its members and in the European venture capital community in general. It has an online directory of its members.

Using the EVCA directory as the only source would have biased the sample as it is well known that it is mostly the larger fund holders that are members of this association. This is the result of the membership fee being quite large compared to those of local organizations. In comparison, very few government fund holders are EVCA members.

Therefore, the EVCA data were supplemented by information from local and national venture capital associations (for instance: the Swedish Venture Capital Association), government website information (for instance: www.anvar.fr) and information from independent parties (for instance: academics, government representatives and so on).

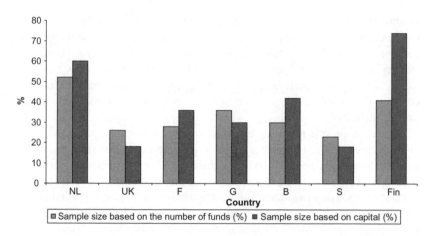

Figure 2.1   Sample of European VCs

We excluded venture capitalists who had not been operating for more than two years and had not made more than 10 investments in early-stage high-tech companies. Given that corporate funds have a very specific investment focus (following up on market trends, for instance), we decided to leave corporate funds out of the analysis. The sample frame consisted of 220 VC funds over the seven selected regions. These were: Île-de-France (France), North-Holland (Netherlands), London–Cambridge region (UK), Flanders (Belgium), Stockholm region (Sweden), Munich region (Germany) and Helsinki region (Finland).

Sixty-eight of these 220 fund holders were interviewed. Figure 2.1 shows the sample representativeness per country.

Given the criticism of earlier methodologies such as *post hoc* and real-time methods, we used conjoint methodology, which builds on the positive aspects of both the *post hoc* and the real-time studies. Based on previous research and interviews with experts, a list of criteria that were important to VCs was compiled. We ended up with four main categories of selection criteria: team, market, product and finance. Following the conjoint methodology, which is often used in marketing research, we ended up with 27 business proposals, which were presented to 68 investment managers and scored by them. Box 2.1 provides an example of such a business proposal. Using conjoint methodology, we derived the importance that investment managers attach to specific selection criteria.

BOX 2.1   EXAMPLE OF A BUSINESS PROPOSAL
         SCORED BY INVESTMENT MANAGERS

You will be presented with a project with the following features:

- The team is NOT COMPLEMENTARY and has NO BUSI-
  NESS EXPERIENCE
- The entrepreneur is a LEADER with PRESEVERANCE,
  with whom you have a GOOD contact
- The company will play on a WORLDWIDE NICHE market
  with HIGH growth potential
- The product is UNIQUE and can be PROTECTED, and is
  ALREADY ACCEPTED by the market
- We can speak of a PLATFORM technology
- We expect break-even AFTER MORE THAN 3 YEARS and
  a return which is LOWER THAN 30%

---

3.   FINDINGS

Our main finding is that European early-stage high-tech investors exhibit heterogeneity in their selection behaviour. Using a hierarchical cluster analysis methodology, we found that three different types of early stage VCs can be distinguished. We call these: (i) technological investors; (ii) people investors; and (iii) financial investors. We found that six decision criteria were significantly different among the groups. First, the importance given to the human resource variables as a reason to invest was significantly different (complementarity of the venture team, competence of the lead entrepreneur and contact with the VC). Second, the market location (local versus global) was significantly different. Third, the importance given to the 'protectability' of the technology characterized certain investors. Finally, the financial part of the deal, such as return on investment, was significantly different. In what follows, the three profiles are illustrated. The figures represent the importance of the different selection criteria to these groups.

3.1   Technology Investors

The first group (32 per cent of all interviewed fund managers) are the technology investors. These VCs put a lot of emphasis on the protectability and the uniqueness of the technology. Also the first contact with the entrepreneur and the relationship they can build with him/her is important. A project is doomed if the VC feels that he/she is not on the same wavelength as the entrepreneur. This indicates that they see themselves more as a financier/entrepreneur. The fact that they do not attach much importance to team characteristics confirms this. The fund investment managers very often have a strong technical profile, and have often obtained a PhD in a technological domain before joining the venture capital industry. This helps them to think in the technical language of the entrepreneur. Furthermore, they can rely on their own network, which is often very much technologically based, to help the entrepreneur. Figure 2.2 represents the importance that this group attributes to each selection criterion. The percentages indicated in the figure indicate what percentage of the final decision is determined by the specific criterion.

As was mentioned before, the protectability of the product and the contact with the entrepreneur have the biggest influence on the investment decision. Furthermore, the foreseen market growth as well as the potential return on investment and the uniqueness of the product are important. So this type of investor really pays attention to a combination of factors, in which the technical characteristics of the product and the contact with the entrepreneur are relatively more important than for the other investors. It is the group of investors that makes the most balanced decision of all investors.

But why do they attach, relatively, so much attention to contact with the entrepreneur? These fund holders invest a lot in teams that are less complementary or in which no commercial experience has been established. In other words, they are assuming that once they have confidence in the technology

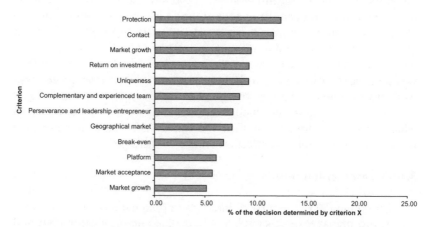

Figure 2.2   Hierarchy of selection criteria of technology investors

and the entrepreneur they: (i) have a better insight into the market opportunities than the actual team members; or (ii) can guide the company enough in order to have an important influence on the financial results.

For this group of investors the criterion of 'market acceptance' comes in at last place. This marks the early phase in which these fund holders are willing to invest; also, in the case when the product has not yet been introduced into the market, they are prepared to provide financing. That is why they attach considerable importance to the uniqueness and the protectability of the product. After all, a company with a protected product will experience less time pressure from potential competitors. This allows these investors to complement the team with their own knowledge or to attract other team members.

Since entrepreneurs looking for finance have no insight into the selection behaviour of the fund holders they are addressing, they can try to assess this selection behaviour on the basis of 'objective' and clearly recognizable characteristics. In what follows we make an attempt to list those characteristics.

Technology investors dispose of relatively more public funding than other funds. This means either that they are completely financed with public capital, or that their shareholders consist of public as well as private parties.

Next, they also invest in the seed phase of the company, which is less the case with other investors in the study. This focus on the seed and early phase is clearly mentioned in their prospectus or on the website. Moreover, most of these fund holders invest more than half of their capital in the early phase of the company.

A bigger proportion of the technology investors also have a socio-economic objective when investing. This means that they not only take financial considerations into account during proposal screening, but they also look at other criteria such as employment, innovation and so on.

Technology investors generally have independent funds, which means that they do not belong to a holding. A fund is considered to be part of a holding if it is part of a group of funds such as follow-up funds or funds with different investment focuses, or if it is set up as a subsidiary (for instance, from a bank). As a matter of fact this group of investors shows a very limited presentation of bank subsidiaries. Smaller VC funds, and often those managing business angel money, are strongly represented.

All of the investment managers in this group have a technical degree. Most of them also have business experience, often in a commercial capacity. This experience has allowed them to develop their network to assist young companies in an early phase. They rarely have experience as an investment manager in other funds. Many of them are making their first moves in the venture capital industry.

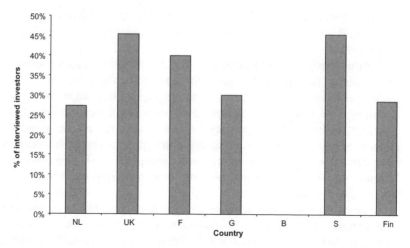

Figure 2.3   Technology investors per country

The geographical focus of these funds is clearly local: investments are made in companies that are localized nearby, in their own region or country. This seems logical considering the big proportion of small VCs in this group.

Figure 2.3 represents an overview of the spread of these funds, which are characterized as technology investors, over the different countries. The absence of Belgian funds within this group is striking. In Box 2.2, we present a profile of one of the VCs interviewed that clearly belonged to this category of technology investors.

3.2 People Investors

Figure 2.4 provides an overview of the selection behaviour of this group of investors (38 per cent of the interviewed fund holders).

This group pays the most attention to human capital factors. The leadership capabilities of the entrepreneur and the quality of his/her team are of overriding importance. Financial criteria come in at second place. However, a lack of quality in the entrepreneurial team of leadership potential can be a breaking point for this group of investors. A business proposal with a team that lacks sufficient experience and that is not complementary has little chance of finding finance with this group of investors. In addition, the contact with the entrepreneur is not really unimportant, but is less pronounced than for the first group of investors (the technology investors). The people investors are those investors who attach the least importance to the protectability of the technology.

BOX 2.2   VENTURE CAPITALIST 1 (UK)

Venture Capitalist 1 was founded in 1984. First, it invested the money of the investment managers (about €2 million). Later, it set up three other funds. The cumulative capital managed in these funds is €90 million. The last fund was raised in 1997 and has €76.5 million under management. This money is invested in high-tech companies that are often still in the phase of product development. Five investment managers manage the fund. Two of them specialize in life sciences, the other three invest in ICT and engineering. Each investment manager follows up on two to four projects. They spend on average one day a week per portfolio company. In order to follow up on their portfolio companies very closely, they mainly invest in the region where they are localized. However, investments abroad are not excluded, but are only made on the condition that the foreign fund takes the lead and follows up on the portfolio company.

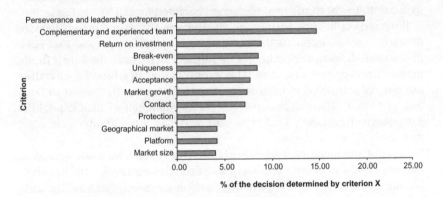

Figure 2.4   Selection criteria of people investors

These investors can also be described as follows: 'Irrespective of the horse (the product), the race (the market) or the odds (the financial criteria), it is the jockey (the entrepreneur) who ultimately determines whether or not the venture capitalist will place a bet'. They assume that an experienced and complementary team can correctly estimate the financial possibilities of the project. Therefore, they have more trust in the financial projections in the business plan. Furthermore, they assume that an experienced team also

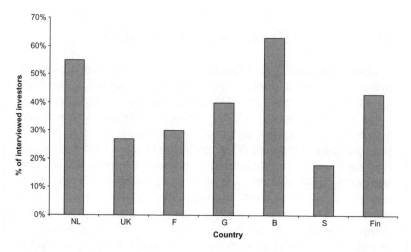

Figure 2.5   Geographical location of the people investors

has insight into the market and knows how to position the product in the marketplace.

Just like the technology investors, the people investors can also be recognized on the basis of some objective characteristics.

With respect to their early-stage investments, this group merely focuses on early-stage investments that have passed the seed stage, and that have also passed the phase of technological uncertainty. They raised their funds mainly from private investors. This group has a very broad focus: they are not only involved in early-stage investments, but often invest in later phases as well. Often, these funds reserve less than half of their capital for early-stage investments. These investors also have a broad interest in non-technological investments.

Most of the investment managers from this group have a non-technical degree, mostly in economics, and have financial experience (in banking, accounting and so on). They are the group of investors that have the least commercial experience. Moreover, it is striking that many of them have worked with other VC funds before joining the fund where they currently work. These investment managers appear to have been in the VC business for the longest time. They mainly invest locally, preferably in their own country.

Figure 2.5 provides an overview of the spread of funds, characterized as people investors, over different countries.

The majority of the interviewed Belgian fund holders can be found in this category, and also many Dutch funds. Generally we can see that most of the funds in continental Europe belong to the group of people investors.

BOX 2.3   VENTURE CAPITALIST 2 (NL)

This VC fund was founded in 1981, and has a cumulative capital of €230 million. In 2004 the VC is investing its fourth fund of €150 million. The fund diversifies its risk by investing in different stages in the high-tech company life cycle. The risk of investing in early-stage high-tech projects is 'compensated' by making investments in later stages and low-tech projects. The VC has a European focus but also invests in Israel. Independent of the type of investment, the VC attaches a high importance to the team that will lead the project and the potential return. Bad scores on these items are an absolute 'no go'. Many of the fund's investment managers had a career in banking before joining the venture capital industry. Many of them have built their experience with other local funds before joining this VC.

In Box 2.3, we present an example of a VC fund that was part of the group of people investors.

3.3   Financial Investors

The third group (30 per cent of the sample) is the group of financial investors, so-called because of the great importance they attach to the financial criteria in the business plan, as Figure 2.6 shows.

This group attaches great importance to the potential return that is stated in the business plan (this is a real breaking point for this group). Also, human factors play an important role. This group invests preferably in well-built teams that are targeting fast-growing markets. Financial investors attach the least importance to contact with the entrepreneur.

The importance that is attached to the potential financial return is strongly linked to the high expectations towards complementarities and experience within the team. Not only do they expect the team to be capable of making a good assessment of the market, on the basis of its own experience and network, but also that the team is able to communicate with other interested parties. They require that the team not only speaks the language of the customer, but also understands the objectives of the VC, which is to make money. Business plans that do not entirely cover the high return requirements of the VC funds give evidence of a lack of sense of reality, and have little chance of finding financing with this group of investors.

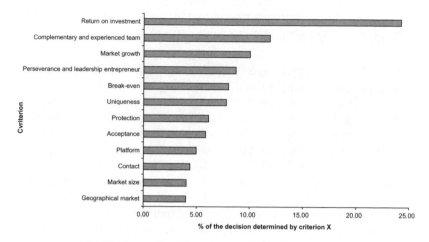

Figure 2.6   Selection criteria of financial investors

Again, there are some objective characteristics observable for this group of investors. They claim to be investing in the seed phase of a company. However, due to the crisis in this sector in past years, only a few investments were effectively made in the seed phase. The percentage of their capital that is invested in the early phase of companies is still much higher compared to the people investors, but is considerably less than the proportion invested by technology investors in this phase.

Financial investors dispose of relatively little public funding, as opposed to the last two groups. It is not surprising that many bank or insurance company subsidiaries are financial investors. The profiles of the investment managers within this group show that they often have a technical degree, as opposed to the second group, where most of the investment managers have an economics background. Many of them have experience in consulting (often at bigger companies such as the Boston Consulting Group and McKinsey). Most of the investment managers have no experience with other funds. Financial investors invest in Europe or worldwide, indicating that they are less restricted in geographical focus than the technology and people investors. Figure 2.7 provides an overview of the spread of those funds, characterized as financial investors, over the different countries.

Belgium and Sweden seem to have a high representation of this type of fund. Also in France many fund holders make their investment decision based mainly on financial criteria. This is not surprising since banks are major providers of venture capital in France. In addition, quite a lot of public money is managed by subsidiaries of banks in this country. Box 2.4 presents an example of a financial investors' VC fund.

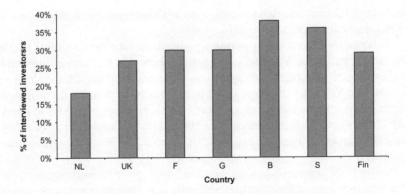

Figure 2.7   Geographical spread of financial investors

BOX 2.4   VENTURE CAPITALIST 3 (F)

This French VC fund is a subsidiary of one of France's largest banks. The fund has been active since 1986 and manages a capital of €500 million. One-quarter of this capital is oriented towards companies that are in their early stage of development. The fund has a specialized sectoral focus, and invests only in ICT. The fund invests mainly in European companies, although investments in US companies are not excluded.

---

4.   CONCLUSION AND IMPLICATIONS

Our results indicate that VCs exhibit substantial heterogeneity in investment selection behaviour. Employing a cluster analysis, three clear types of investors emerge: those who focus on technology, those who focus on finance and those who focus on people. We then examined differences among the three groups in terms of their sectoral focus, the sources of funds and the human capital of the investment manager. The results indicate that technology investors make most use of public money. These funds often employ investment managers with a technical background who have experience in the academic world. Financial investors make the least use of public capital. Their investment managers often built their experience in consulting and only rarely have experience within other funds. People investors do not invest exclusively in early-stage high-tech proposals but diversify the risk by investing in non-tech later-stage proposals. Their investment managers often have experience within other VC funds and have a business education.

This research has some important implications for practitioners. First, it has implications for VC funds. The results show that the background and experience of investment managers can influence the individual's selection behaviour. VCs may therefore build their investment teams with a human capital consideration in mind. In addition, it is interesting for VCs to know which VCs have similar selection patterns and thus to know which VCs they will be competing with on specific deals, or could be potential syndication partners.

Second, this research has implications for high-tech entrepreneurs. So far, research has studied venture capitalists as if they were a homogeneous group of investors. The fact that this research focuses only on early-stage high-tech investing makes it even more interesting to this group of entrepreneurs who are looking for finance for their early-stage high-tech project, and who are less interested in knowing how later-stage and non-tech investors select their investments. Entrepreneurs can benefit from a better knowledge of what drives selection behaviour, and thus approach those investors who are more likely to invest in their project. This may increase his/her chances of finding the appropriate investor for the business proposal. It is particularly interesting to the entrepreneur to know that selection behaviour differs between funds and that not all VCs are putting the same criteria on top of their list. In addition, it is interesting for the entrepreneur to understand how fund characteristics, the background of the investment manager, and the sector the investment proposal is in, will determine the VC's selection behaviour. This research shows, for instance, that business proposals with weaker entrepreneurial teams but a strong technology may still stand a chance when looking for finance with, for example, publicly financed funds.

Third, this research has important implications for fund investors, and more specifically investors of public money. The results indicate that public money is used for investing in business proposals with a strong technological basis. This may be viewed as an attempt to overcome problems associated with perceived market failures, which exist for early-stage high-tech funding.

REFERENCES

Hisrich, R.D. and Jankowitz, A.D. (1990), 'Intuition in venture capital decisions: an exploratory study using a new technique', *Journal of Business Venturing*, **5**, 49–62.
Lockett, A., Murray, G. and Wright, M. (2002), 'Do UK venture capitalists still have a bias against investment in new technology firms?', *Research Policy*, **31**, 1009–30.

MacMillan, I.C., Siegel, R. and Subbanarashima, P.N. (1985), 'Criteria used by venture capitalists to evaluate new venture proposals', *Journal of Business Venturing*, **1**, 119–28.

MacMillan, I.C., Zemann, L. and Subbanarashima, P.N. (1987), 'Criteria distinguishing successful from unsuccessful ventures in the venture screening process', *Journal of Business Venturing*, **2**, 123–37.

Muzyka, D., Birley, S. and Leleux, B. (1996), 'Trade-offs in the investment decisions of European venture capitalists', *Journal of Business Venturing*, **11**, 273–87.

Shepherd, D.A. and Zacharakis, A. (1998), 'Conjoint analysis: a new methodological approach for researching the decision policies of venture capitalists', *Venture Capital*, **1**(3), 197–217.

Tyebjee, T.T. and Bruno, A.V. (1984), 'A model of VC investment activity', *Management Science*, **30**, 1051–66.

3. Private equity investors, corporate governance and professionalization

Christof Beuselinck, Sophie Manigart and Tom Van Cauwenberge

1. INTRODUCTION

Private equity (PE) has developed as an important financing mechanism for firms where traditional financing alternatives are insufficiently accessible or impossible to obtain. PE in the sense of venture capital, which is typically provided to young and small firms without sufficient track records and assets in-place, fills the void between sources of funds for innovation and traditional financing alternatives. In a broader sense, PE also represents external equity capital that is raised to strengthen a company's balance sheet, to make acquisitions or to finance a management buy-out or buy-in. Hence, PE is an instrument which complements established financing alternatives like bank and other credits on the one hand and stock markets on the other. It fulfils a vital task in contemporary capital markets by enabling firms to obtain the necessary capital to develop, run and expand their businesses.

Unlike most intermediate finance mechanisms, PE combines the provision of finance with active governance and control in their portfolio firms. Thus, by raising PE, entrepreneurs can finance their businesses and in addition obtain a spell of professional management skills and supportive guidance. This combination allows businesses to achieve a higher level of professionalism. Public authorities like the Organization for Economic Cooperation and Development (OECD) and the European Union (EU) are increasingly convinced of the key role that PE encompasses in the overall business development of a region or country and stimulate its development actively. The specific nature and unique characteristics, which are inherently attached to PE as a financing technique, has resulted in multiple studies focusing on the nature and attributes of the PE investment process.

Despite the numerous PE studies that have been carried out until now, questions still remain about how entrepreneurs attract PE investors' attention in the pre-investment period, how PE investors monitor and control their portfolio firms and to what extent these efforts influence the corporate governance system in-place, and finally to what extent PE investors' involvement affects their portfolio firms' further development and professionalization. The above-mentioned aspects need further consideration to better map the entrepreneurial–PE investor mutual relationship and the impact this has on corporate governance frameworks, internal professionalization practice and the interplay between both in portfolio firms.

In this chapter, we present results of a unique study that tackles these issues both in a qualitative and quantitative way. In-depth interviews are conducted on a selected sample of 16 later-stage PE investors, active in the Continental European market, to gauge the monitoring extent and interference of PE investors in their portfolio firms' operational and financial business processes. This research technique yields in-depth information on how PE investors monitor and control their participation. In Section 3, we present additional results of a large sample quantitative study that measures the effect of the PE monitoring mechanisms on the quality and quantity of the financial reporting of portfolio firms. As such, this study is one of the first to combine the real monitoring efforts of PE investors and the measurable effects of intensified governance on the professionalism of the financial reporting of their firms under portfolio. Providing more insight and uncovering general trends in this relationship helps both professionals and academics to a better understanding of the way in which PE deals are controlled and monitored *ex post* as well as what effects this extensive monitoring entails for portfolio firms' professionalization profile.

This study is unique in that it complements existing research that has traditionally been carried out in the US venture capital industry. By studying characteristics of and trends in the relation between entrepreneurs and PE investors in a Continental European context (namely Belgium), we cover not only a different geographical market but also a more extensive investment spectrum (that is, early-stage venture capital as well as later-stage PE) than traditionally has been analysed in US studies. Moreover, the data used in the analyses allow us to confront differences in monitoring and controlling techniques dependent on PE investors' origin. This adds an additional dimension to the research by incorporating differences in geographical and institutional culture. The data used in the current study also allow us to explore an often ignored element in PE research, namely whether monitoring and professionalization is driven by investor type. We therefore study differences in reporting professionalism and quality dependent on whether a public or a private investor backs a portfolio firm.

2. HOW DO PE INVESTORS MONITOR THEIR PORTFOLIO COMPANIES?

We conducted 16 in-depth interviews with later-stage PE investors, all active in the Belgian market but which have British, Dutch, French or purely Belgian backgrounds. Previous studies have shown that the UK and the Netherlands have better developed less rigid financial markets, more widely-held capital and ownership structures and a better investor protection rights system compared to France and Belgium. Seven of the interviewed PE investors have their corporate headquarter in the UK or the Netherlands while nine are based in Belgium or France. We refer to the former group as Anglo-Saxon-type countries and the latter as Continental European countries. All are active in the Belgian market. As such, this dataset allows to study differences and similarities in monitoring and corporate governance systems depending on investor origin (Anglo-Saxon versus Continental European investors).

We opted for qualitative interviews since these enable us to gain comprehensible insights into the way PE investors monitor and control their portfolio firms. The general objective of these interviews was to obtain reflections upon the monitoring and control of successful versus poorly performing firms and recently obtained versus older participations in which the fund has a substantial equity stake.

In general, results of these interviews indicate that PE investors use extensive monitoring devices to control and follow-up their portfolio firms. PE investors can control their portfolio firms through: (i) the board of directors; (ii) interim reporting; (iii) internal/external audits; and (iv) *ad hoc* communication with management team members. However, differences between Anglo-Saxon and Continental European PE investors are striking with respect to both the frequency and the intensity by which these devices are applied.

2.1 Board of Directors

The board of directors is an organism active at the top of a company with a variety of tasks and duties. The board not only overviews the organization of the administration and operations and financial matters but also takes strategic decisions, organizes mergers and acquisitions (M&A) arrangements, elects the president and decides upon salaries and payment policies of personnel and top management. Most PE investors appoint a representative on the board of directors to gain control of their portfolio firms' policies and activities, but Anglo-Saxon PE investors do this more frequently than Continental European investors.

All except one Anglo-Saxon PE investor always appoint a board representative while only two out of three Continental European investors do this. Further, the frequency of board meetings is considerably higher for Anglo-Saxon compared to Continental European PE investors. Whereas the former typically have a meeting once a month (with the exception of the summer period), the latter meet only once every two to three months. In both groups, the frequency of board meetings is higher the more recent the firm is under portfolio. Further, board members appointed by Anglo-Saxon PE investors often play an informative role whereas board members of Continental European PE investors have a more restrictive and decision-making power.

Generally, board members appointed by PE investors play a dominant value-added role. By and large, PE investors appoint financially skilled people who often come from their own investment company or are acquaintances, to introduce the necessary financial expertise. If board representatives are not predominantly financially skilled, they typically have experience either in the industry-specific complexity or with respect to general management. This shows that PE investors' monitoring and control are closely related to the extent of professionalization. Not only do PE investors monitor their investments closely by appointing independent board members but they also indirectly elevate the firm at a higher professionalization level through active interventions in the company's management.

2.2 Interim Reporting

Through interim reporting, PE investors require a quantifiable output of the company's performance and financial health between board meetings. The interim reporting required by the PE investor may, but does not necessarily, equal the information that goes to the board of directors. For Anglo-Saxon PE investors, the reporting is indeed the same for both purposes, although for Continental European PE investors this is only the same in half of the cases. It should be noted that the substantially longer time period between two consecutive board meetings in the Continental European sample undoubtedly drives this relation. Interestingly, less successful participations are compelled to report information more often than more successful entities.

The information content of the interim reports mainly relates to order book, cash flow and liquidity figures. To facilitate the monitoring and decision-making process, the information should be available in good time. In nearly all cases (14 out of 16), portfolio firms are able to present the interim reporting in less than two weeks. Further, an adequate control of the portfolio firms not only requires timely, but also accurate information. For successful participations, PE investors label the accuracy of the reporting as 'excellent' or at least 'satisfactory'. For less successful participations, PE investors describe the reporting accuracy more often as 'medium' or 'poor'.

2.3 Audit Certification

Another means by which PE investors can monitor and control their participations is through internal and external audits. PE investors often appoint an external auditor to attest the true and fair view of the portfolio firm's statutory financial accounts. In the Anglo-Saxon sample, the task of the external auditors is more extensive in that they also verify the management reporting. Tasks of external auditors of Continental European PE investors encompass the attestation neither of management reports nor of operational key performance indicators. Continental European PE investors often mention the word 'trust' as a rationale for why the external audit does not cover these issues.

The installation of an internal audit committee, however, is not common practice. Six of the interviewed PE investors never install audit committees in their portfolio firms, eight do appoint a committee, but only in a minority of their participations, and only two have an audit committee in more than half of their participations. There is no structural difference between Continental European and Anglo-Saxon investors. Most commonly cited reasons for having an audit committee are (i) the historical presence of an internal audit committee before the PE investment and (ii) the company size, that is, whether or not a company exceeds specific thresholds with respect to sales levels and number of employees. The task of this audit committee is limited to verifying the accuracy of the statutory financial statements and usually does not entail verification of management reports.

Remarkably, in only four out of the 16 cases, PE investors have an internal back office that is authorized to audit the portfolio firms rigorously. The tasks of this back office vary from reviewing the financial reporting to performing operational audits and providing assistance in specific projects (for example, Enterprise Resource Planning (ERP) implementation). The existence of the back office unit is unrelated to PE investor origin, size or investment focus.

2.4 *Ad Hoc* Communication

PE investors typically also keep an eye on their participations by means of formal and informal *ad hoc* communication with members of the management team. Anglo-Saxon PE investors have weekly contact with the chief executive officer (CEO) of successful participations and even daily contact with those of less successful firms. By contrast, Continental European PE investors contact the CEOs of their successful participations only once a month and the average contacting frequency is weekly if things go bad. Informal contacts with the chief financial officer (CFO) of the portfolio firms show similar patterns to those with the CEO. Anglo-Saxon PE investors communicate more frequently with their portfolio firm's CFO than do Continental European PE investors.

Further, Anglo-Saxon PE investors have contact with other management team members such as the operational manager or the human resource manager while Continental European PE investors tend to avoid contacts with managers other than the CEO and the CFO. The reasons behind this behaviour are: (i) PE investors consider themselves not to have adequate knowledge to become involved with managers other than the CEO/CFO; and (ii) PE investors do not want to bypass the CEO/CFO. This finding further highlights the intrinsic differences between both Anglo-Saxon and Continental European PE investors.

In summary, the findings of the interviews confirm the overall belief that active monitoring and control is a key issue to prevent agency problems between PE investors and entrepreneurs. Monitoring finds a place through a variety of control mechanisms: PE investors appoint representatives on the portfolio firm's board of directors, require interim reporting, have face-to-face communications with the management team, establish internal audit committees and appoint statutory external auditors. There are, however, substantial differences in monitoring and control strategies between Anglo-Saxon and Continental European PE investors. Anglo-Saxon PE investors tend to consult more management team members than Continental European ones and do not avoid contact with operational team experts. Moreover, Anglo-Saxon investors have more frequent informal contacts with members of the management team than their Continental European counterparts. One issue that corresponds most between both PE investor groups is the central focus on financial information. PE investors state that operational information is subordinate and is received only on a scattered basis. One PE investor even commented: 'If there's no reason to ask operational questions, why bother? We are not operational experts . . . We don't care if it doesn't impact the financial figures and we don't look at it until there's an issue'. Figure 3.1 shows an overview of the diverse monitoring and control mechanisms that PE investors impose on their portfolio firms.

Board of Directors

Anglo-Saxon type	Continental European type
Nearly always represented Frequent meeting (1/month) Financial, industry-specific or general management skills	Often represented Less frequent meeting (1/quarter) Financial, industry-specific or general management skills

Interim Reporting

Anglo-Saxon type	Continental European type
Same information as reported to board of directors Less successful participations: more frequent interim reporting Reporting is of a lower accuracy for poorly performing participations	Often other information than that reported to board of directors Less successful participations: more frequent interim reporting Reporting is less accurate for poorly performing participations

Ad Hoc Communication

Anglo-Saxon type	Continental European type
Successful participations: weekly contacts Poorly performing participations: daily contacts Contact CEO, CFO and other management team members	Successful participations: monthly/occasional contacts Poorly performing participations: weekly contacts Contact CEO, CFO and avoid others

Audit Certification (Internal & External)

Anglo-Saxon type	Belgium type
Audit committees: not frequently installed tasks = limited to statutory accounts External auditor: commonly appointed statutory accounts	Audit committees: not frequently installed tasks = limited to statutory accounts External auditor: commonly appointed statutory accounts & management reports

Figure 3.1   Monitoring and control devices

3. IMPACT OF PE MONITORING ON THE QUALITY OF FINANCIAL REPORTS

This section examines the impact of PE investor monitoring and control on their portfolio firms' financial reporting quality. The quality of financial reporting is an issue that has often been neglected in entrepreneurial research but that is important for a broad group of stakeholders such as providers of finance (banks and other third parties), customers, employees and the government, but also for PE investors. The abundance of accounting scandals that have recently come to light shows that stakeholders can easily become victims of managers who report misleading financial results in an attempt to maximize their own profit and wealth. Not only have unscrupulous businesspeople providing over optimistic company results cheated numerous investors, but also banks have suffered high losses since these companies often went bankrupt. This forced banks to incorporate high write-offs on defaulted loans, bringing themselves closer to potential demise. As a further consequence, numerous employees have been laid off. Since the quality and accuracy of financial reporting clearly is important for a broad range of stakeholders, it is relevant to study the impact that PE investors have on the financial statement information quality of their portfolio firms.

In order to conduct a study on portfolio firms' reporting quality, we personally investigated a sample of over 800 Belgian firms that received PE financing between 1985 and 1999. We checked PE investment reports, press releases and annual statements to draw up this comprehensive sample. We obtained financial statement information data from the National Bank of Belgium, the identification of the PE investor and the proportion of the share capital that PE investors obtain. Portfolio companies that are financial institutions and banks are excluded from the analyses because of their highly specific characteristics. This resulted in a final sample of 556 firms backed by PE investors: 37 per cent of the firms that receive PE financing are younger than two years at the time of the PE financing; 18 per cent are between two and five years; and 45 per cent are older than five years.

The financial reporting quality of these firms is evaluated and compared to that of a comparable sample of firms that are matched in size, age and industry type. Statistical tests have been performed to verify the robustness of the matching procedure and the precision of the results. We study the previously unexplored question of whether PE investors have an impact on the financial reporting quality of their portfolio firms and hence professionalize the financial reporting environment. This is an important issue since academic research has shown that firms providing reliable and high-quality financial information can benefit from enhanced contract terms and lower capital costs. The quality of the financial reporting is measured by the extent of earnings management and earnings conservatism, and by the disclosure of information.

3.1 Earnings Management

Earnings management is a widely studied topic in financial accounting research and relates to the extent of reporting flexibility and discretion that managers use in their earnings reporting. Managers can, for example, stretch or shrink the accounts payable (or receivable, respectively) time, alter depreciation policies, shift debt from the balance sheet by creating special purpose entities or apply extensive discretion in revaluing assets. Earnings management is not bad *per se* since it might contain inside information that managers reveal by exploiting their financial reporting discretion. Most studies, however, conclude that earnings management is negatively related to the financial reporting quality. Numerous recent cases show that earnings management is often used for aggressively overstating revenues and understating expenses in an attempt to present euphemistic company results.

We study whether earnings management behaviour of entrepreneurial firms is related to receiving PE in the years both before and after the investment. We are specifically interested in whether entrepreneurs apply earnings management techniques to attract the interest of PE investors and whether the earnings management flexibility is reduced after investment in terms of the PE investor's monitoring.

Results of univariate and multivariate earnings management tests show that PE-backed firms have a higher level of earnings management in the pre-financing years than non-PE-backed equivalents. Whereas the measurable earnings management component grows from 2.15 per cent of total assets two years before PE financing to 4.00 per cent in the financing year, it is close to zero for the matched sample years. This suggests that entrepreneurs searching for PE financing apply earnings management techniques to boost their results. Although PE investors are sophisticated investment parties and will most likely see through this kind of earnings management, the finding might not be that surprising. Entrepreneurs can decide to apply earnings management to boost their company results, thereby hoping to attract the attention of potential investors. Results further show that this aggressive upward earnings management evaporates entirely in the post-financing years, suggesting that active PE involvement and intensified monitoring techniques reduce earnings management possibilities for portfolio firms.

3.2   Earnings Conservatism

Earnings conservatism is an alternative measure for earnings quality and relates to the prudence by which financial results are reported. Firms that disclose losses promptly instead of smoothing their negative results over a number of consecutive years are labelled as more conservative firms. Firms may prefer a smoother earnings pattern since this typically is associated with less risk. Recent studies have shown that listed firms report more conservative earnings than unlisted firms, suggesting that the higher demand for timely information by the stock market is reflected in a higher willingness to disclose losses punctually. Since PE investors typically want to identify potential pitfalls immediately and the interview results show that their influence on the financial reporting of their participations is substantial, portfolio firms are expected to recognize losses more quickly than similar firms where no such PE governance is practised.

Results of multivariate earnings conservatism regression analyses show that PE-backed firms have a higher tendency to report losses in good time compared to non-PE-backed equivalents from the PE financing year onwards. Hence, the results suggest that PE investor presence is associated not only with lower earnings management levels but also with higher earnings conservatism. Further, portfolio firms of government-related PE investors recognize losses less quickly than portfolio firms of non-government-related PE investors. The often-documented lower degree of professionalism and active monitoring that are associated with government-related PE investors seem to influence the earnings quality of their portfolio firms, at least with respect to earnings conservatism.

3.3   Disclosure of Financial Information

Another important attribute of financial reporting quality is a firm's willingness to disclose information to outsiders above the statutory minima. Disclosure research has identified various determinants of firms' disclosure policies and multiple economic benefits associated with increased disclosure. In line with the postulation that entrepreneurs try to catch the attention of outside PE investors by overstating their reported earnings, they can additionally decide to disclose more information to outsiders to reduce information asymmetries. This higher disclosure is likely to be evaluated positively by the PE investor as it reflects a higher professionalism and willingness to share information before and after the PE investment deal. We study portfolio firms' disclosure behaviour by looking at tendencies to report complete financial statements although legally, abbreviated financial statements are sufficient. Reporting complete financial statements induces

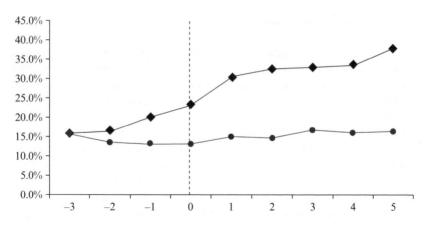

Figure 3.2   Proportion of high disclosure firms

higher preparation and presentation costs and also exacerbates the competitive situation since it provides industry competitors with a substantial amount of useful information such as sales levels and cost structures.

Figure 3.2 shows the proportional evolution of firms that voluntarily report complete financial statements (that is, high disclosure firms) in a time window of three years before to six years after the initial PE investment. Univariate and multivariate panel logit tests show that PE portfolio firms disclose significantly more financial information than legally required from the pre-investment year onwards.

On average, 15 per cent of the companies that are not financed by PE investors report complete financial statements although abbreviated statements are sufficient. Figure 3.2 shows that this percentage rises to 20 per cent for firms that search for PE in the pre-investment year. After having received PE, this percentage increases further to more than 30 per cent. These results suggest that (i) firms looking for PE voluntarily disclose more information than legally required to signal their quality to outsiders (including potential PE investors) and (ii) PE investor presence leads to a higher disclosure policy. The latter finding is interesting in that it further illustrates that PE investors help to elevate the financial reporting professionalism of portfolio firms to a higher level, consistent with the behaviour reported in the interviews. It might also be an indication of PE investors preparing their portfolio firms for a future exit. Increased disclosure is one means to reduce information asymmetries or signal quality and professionalism to prospective buyers of the firm. There are no differences in post-PE investment disclosure behaviour for different investor types. Unlike the results of earnings conservatism regressions, we find no clear relation between the type of PE investor and portfolio firms' disclosure policy.

In summary, these quantitative findings show comprehensible extra evidence that PE investor involvement affects the reported earnings quality in a variety of ways. Lower earnings management, more timely loss reporting and higher disclosure reflect the professionalization impact of PE investors on their portfolio firms. This multi-method research is one of the first to quantify measurable effects of PE involvement on at least one aspect of their professionalism, namely the quality and quantity of their financial reporting.

4. CONCLUSION AND IMPLICATIONS

It is well known that PE investors actively monitor and control their participation to detect problems early and to reduce the probability that entrepreneurs act in their own, rather than the company's, interest. However, questions still remain as to how this monitoring finds a place in practice and whether different investors behave differently. Moreover, it is unclear whether, and if so to what extent, this monitoring affects the corporate governance in place and the professionalization of their portfolio firms. This multi-method study is one of the first to tackle these challenging issues jointly by combining interview results with quantitative data.

We find that PE investors monitor their portfolio firms through different channels. They intervene actively through the board of directors, require regular interim reports, communicate frequently with management team members and can install both an internal audit committee and external auditors to certify the accounting figures. Audit committees and audits by the back office, however, are infrequently used monitoring tools. We find that the focus of all control mechanisms is on the accounting and financial figures, rather than the operational issues.

PE investor origin determines both the frequency and intensity of monitoring. Anglo-Saxon PE investors are more involved on the board of directors, have more frequent contacts with management team members and contact more members of the team than Continental European investors. Moreover, they require external auditors not to limit their job to purely certifying the statutory accounts but also to check the management reporting. Continental European investors, however, do not require the latter. The findings clearly hint that differences in cultural background and origin-related preferences affect the way PE investors approach and monitor their portfolio firms. Monitoring intensity decreases both with the time a firm is in the PE investor's portfolio and with its performance.

Further, we find large sample evidence that PE investors add value to their portfolio firms by improving the quality and disclosure extent of their portfolio firms' financial reporting. As such, this study is one of the first to provide empirical evidence that PE investors positively influence at least one aspect of the professionalization of portfolio firms, namely they improve the quality and quantity of their financial reporting. This clearly confirms that PE investors perform tasks in their portfolio firms that go beyond those of traditional financial intermediaries.

This study has important implications for entrepreneurs, PE investors and other stakeholders of PE-backed firms. From an entrepreneurial perspective, it is clear that opting for PE finance is inherently connected with a high degree of monitoring once PE investors are on board. However, this tight monitoring should not necessarily be interpreted negatively since portfolio firms benefit from the PE investors' presence in several ways: they gain financial and general expertise and build financial discipline and professionalism. Further, our results are also important for other stakeholders of PE-backed firms since they show that such firms have more reliable, more conservative and more extensive financial reporting once PE investors are involved. Hence, PE investors' presence drives the financial reporting quality of portfolio firms positively. Finally, our study is important in that we show that Continental European investors monitor their portfolio firms less tightly and they are less concerned with operational issues. This finding might partly explain the higher return of Anglo-Saxon PE investment funds compared to their Continental European colleagues.

REFERENCES

Ball, R. and Shivakumar, L. (2005), 'Earnings quality in private UK companies: comparative loss recognition timeliness', *Journal of Accounting and Economics*, **39**, 83–128.

Beuselinck, C., Deloof, M. and Manigart, S. (2004a), 'Private equity and earnings quality', Working Paper Series Ghent University, 04/221, 47 pp.

Beuselinck, C., Deloof, M. and Manigart, S. (2004b), 'Private equity investments and disclosure policy', Working Paper Series Ghent University, 42 pp.

Gompers, P.A. (1995), 'Optimal investment, monitoring, and the staging of venture capital', *Journal of Finance*, **50** (5), 1461–89.

Kaplan, S.N. and Strömberg, P. (2004), 'Characteristics, contracts, and actions: evidence from venture capitalist analyses', *Journal of Finance*, **59** (5), 2177–209.

Teoh, S.H., Welch, I. and Wong, T.J. (1998), 'Earnings management and the long-run market performance of initial public offerings', *Journal of Finance*, **53** (6), 1935–74.

4. The impact of capital inflows and management skills on the performance of European private equity funds

Christoph Kaserer and Christian Diller

1. INTRODUCTION

In this chapter we address two important topics concerning the performance of European private equity funds. First, we discuss briefly how the performance of a private equity fund should be measured. On that basis we offer some performance data for mature European private equity funds. Second, we raise the question what factors have an impact on these returns. In this regard we put special emphasis on two specific issues, known in the literature as the persistence and money-chasing-deals phenomena. In this chapter we present strong evidence in favour of the existence of both of these phenomena, which has important consequences for investors allocating a part of their wealth under management towards the private equity industry.

It is well known that there are many different ways to measure returns of private equity funds. First, the industry itself mostly relies on an internal rate of return approach (IRR) or, even simpler, on a multiple approach. An important argument against using the IRR as a return measure relates to the fact that it is assumed that the opportunity cost of capital invested in the fund is equal to the IRR. As the investment opportunities of a private equity fund may be rather singular, this makes little sense. Moreover, in this way any comparison with other asset classes is subject to distortion. Due to these shortcomings another performance measure has been proposed: the public market equivalent approach (PME). Basically, under this approach the simplifying assumption is made that the opportunity cost of a private equity investment is equal to the rate of return of a public market benchmark.

An even more interesting question relates to factors explaining the performance of an investment in a private equity fund. In frictionless and perfectly competitive capital markets we would expect returns of private equity funds to be determined by systematic risk only. Neither personal skills of the management team, that is, the general partner (GP), nor the inflow of money into private equity funds should have an impact on the performance of these funds. This is because of rational expectations and perfect competitiveness governing the pricing in financing rounds, that is, the valuation of all the potential investment projects. The assumption of perfect capital markets is, of course, very far-reaching, and there is ample evidence that even on organized and liquid stock markets pricing phenomena arise that are not completely in line with this assumption.

One might therefore expect that with respect to private equity markets the assumption of perfect capital markets is rather heroic. This is due to the specific characteristics of the private equity asset class, for example, the illiquidity of an investment, the stickiness of fund flows, the restricted number of target companies and the segmentation from other asset classes. That is why the market may be far from being frictionless and perfectly competitive, at least in the short run. Gompers and Lerner (2000) presented a very important finding in this regard. They showed that inflows into venture funds and target companies' valuations correlate positively. If real-life private equity markets adopt the above-described characteristics, we would expect that realized returns of private equity funds are also affected by total capital inflows in the industry. More specifically, the money-chasing-deals phenomenon would suggest that there should be a negative correlation between a fund's performance and the amount of capital directed towards the private equity industry. This, however, would only be true to the extent that fund inflows are not matched by an improvement in economic perspectives of ultimate target companies. In this chapter we propose a test for the money-chasing-deals phenomenon that basically relies on the fact that we make a distinction between absolute and relative cash inflows into private equity funds. We can show that for a given absolute fund inflow, an increase in the allocation of money towards a particular fund type has a significant negative impact on the performance of this fund type. This finding strongly supports the money-chasing-deals phenomenon.

Additionally, we analyse whether the skills of a fund management team have an impact on the return of this particular fund. If this persistence phenomenon exists, returns of all funds managed by the same team should have a positive correlation. In our empirical study, we find returns to be positively associated with GPs' skills.

2.   DESCRIPTION OF THE DATASET USED

The empirical results of this chapter are based on a large dataset provided by the European Venture Capital and Private Equity Association (EVCA) and Thomson Venture Economics (TVE). It consists of 777 European private equity funds with vintage years from 1980 to 2003. The idea in the empirical part of our approach is to get rid of the net asset value (NAV) bias by inferring the performance of the private equity fund only on the basis of realized cash flows. In a very strict sense, this would allow us to analyse liquidated funds only. However, only 95 funds in the dataset have already been liquidated and have an average age of about 12.6 years. As we observed that more recently founded funds have an above average return, looking at liquidated funds only would clearly cause a negative selection bias because more recent vintage years would be underrepresented in our sample. Hence, we increase the dataset by adding mature funds, that is, funds with a relatively small NAV, because for those funds valuation biases should have a small impact on performance recordings. The restriction was that the residual NAV of such a fund is not higher than 10 per cent (sample I) or 20 per cent (sample II) of the undiscounted absolute sum of all previously accrued cash flows. Formally, we integrated a non-liquidated fund in samples I and II, respectively, if it met the following condition:

$$\frac{RNAV_N}{\sum_{t=0}^{N}|CF_t|} \leq q \Leftrightarrow \frac{1 + DPI_N}{RVPI_N} \geq \frac{1}{q}.$$

This ratio could be interpreted as the cash flow determined age of the fund. For these funds the residual NAV is treated as a fictive distribution accruing at the end of June 2003. Using these criteria we get two new samples with 200 (sample I) and 262 (sample II) funds, respectively. Although this approach may suffer from a selection bias as well, it should be noted that we pick out those funds that either already paid very high cash flows (positive selection) or had to reduce their NAV considerably (negative selection). The distribution of the vintage years of our funds is described in Figure 4.1.

3. PERFORMANCE MEASURES FOR EUROPEAN PRIVATE EQUITY FUNDS

In this section we present the results with respect to the return distribution of European private equity funds. It should be noted here first, that there is an ongoing debate on how to measure the return distribution of an illiquid investment. This is especially important if one is interested in asset allocation decisions. The IRR is the common performance measure in the private equity industry. However, as the shortcomings of the IRR are well

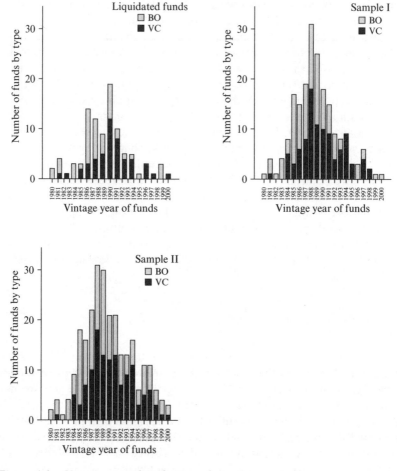

Figure 4.1   Vintage year distribution of our three samples

known we use an alternative performance measure in our study: the public
market equivalent.

3.1   IRRs of European Private Equity Funds

Using this European dataset we get the results presented in Table 4.1. The
pooled average IRR, that is, the average of all funds in our data sample,
is 10 per cent for liquidated funds, while the IRRs for our extended
samples I and II are on a perceivably higher level of 13 and 14 per cent,
respectively. This result has to be compared with the result reported by

Table 4.1   Pooled sample distribution of IRRs of European private equity funds (%)

IRR(CF)	VC	BO	Total
Liquidated funds			
Average	7.32	12.64	10.01
Median	4.77	9.79	7.28
75th percentile	12.98	18.67	14.24
25th percentile	−4.00	8.23	0.00
Std dev.	17.82	17.67	17.85
Sample I			
Average	12.00	13.39	12.69
Median	8.05	10.80	9.14
75th percentile	15.65	18.76	17.13
25th percentile	1.90	9.00	4.45
Std dev.	22.06	16.18	19.34
Sample II			
Average	12.50	15.63	14.07
Median	7.40	11.00	9.56
75th percentile	16.31	19.95	18.17
25th percentile	0.00	1.69	0.05
Std dev.	24.95	20.59	22.89

Kaplan and Schoar (2005) for US funds, where they found an average IRR of 17 per cent. The distribution of the IRR is heavily skewed as can be seen from the relatively low medians as well as from the very high first quartile levels. In fact, 25 per cent of the funds in sample I generated an IRR that was not lower than 17 per cent. Moreover, Table 4.1 corroborates the view that in terms of IRR European buy-out (BO) funds performed considerably better than European venture capital (VC) funds. Finally, it should be noted that the variability of the IRR increases when the dataset is enlarged. This is in accordance with our presumption that our method picks out successful as well as poor-performing funds.

3.2   Benchmarking Returns by Using the PME Approach

In order to benchmark IRRs it is often proposed to use an excess IRR, defined as the IRR of a single fund minus the return on a benchmark index over the fund's lifetime. The average excess IRR for European private equity funds in contrast to the Morgan Stanley Capital International Inc. (MSCI) Europe is about 4.45 per cent for our sample I.

The PME approach addresses the question of how much money a private equity investor would need in order to generate a cash flow stream with a public market investment equal to the cash flow stream generated by the private equity investment. A PME of 1.2 informs the investor that for every euro invested in the private equity fund he/she needs €1.2 to be invested in the benchmark index in order to generate the same cash flow stream. This is equivalent to the comparison of the following two investment strategies. Under strategy 1 the investor starts with a given amount of euros that is exactly sufficient for financing all take-downs, under the assumption that the money not used for immediate take-downs is invested in the benchmark index until it is called by the GP. Simultaneously, the distributions paid to the investor are immediately invested in the index. In this way the investor is left with a final wealth at the maturity of the fund. Under strategy 2 the same amount of euros is immediately invested in the benchmark index with a maturity equal to the fund's lifetime. The PME is nothing more than the ratio of the final wealth under the first strategy to the final wealth under the second strategy. More formally, the PME is defined as follows:

$$PME = \frac{\sum_{t=1}^{T} cf_t \prod_{i=t+1}^{T}(1 + R_{Ii})}{\prod_{t=1}^{T}(1 + R_{It})}.$$

Here, R_{It} is the net return on a public benchmark index in period t, while cf_t is the normalized distribution (positive cash flow) of a private equity fund in period t. The distributions are normalized by dividing them with the present value of all investments, that is, the present value of all take-downs (negative cash flows). In this way the cash flows are normalized to an initial investment with a present value of €1, where the benchmark index return is used as the discount rate.

Evidently, the PME approach can be used for an *ex post* benchmarking. In this case the known cash flows of a fund as well as the known benchmark returns are used for calculating the PME according to the above formula. By using the MSCI Europe as well as the JP Morgan European Government Bond Index as benchmarks (this index is available only from 1993. As we need a longer index history we use the German REXP index for periods before 1993. The REXP is a performance index of German treasury bonds over the whole maturity range), we get the results for our pooled sample presented in Table 4.2. (One remark concerning the comparison of the private equity returns calculated on cash flows basis (net of management fees) with the returns of the indices. As we can observe only the returns on a market index that are gross of management fees, we shall make the following correction in this empirical study: for an equity index we assume management fees to be equal to 50 basis points (bps) per year, while for a bond index these fees are assumed to be equal to 20 bps. Hence, the net yearly return is equal to the gross yearly return, as indicated by the index performance, times 0.995 and 0.998, respectively. In this chapter the MSCI Europe is used as an equity index and the JP Morgan European Government as a bond index.)

Two results should be emphasized here. First, when using the MSCI Europe as the benchmark we find a PME smaller than 1 for the sample of liquidated funds as well as for sample I. This is in contrast to the positive result of the excess IRR. Evidently, the excess IRR and the IRR of a fund is not a suitable method for benchmarking returns. Second, by comparing returns of VC and BO funds, Table 4.2 indicates that the ranking depends on the subsample as well as on the benchmark used. This is again in clear contrast to the results derived on the basis of the IRR in Table 4.1, where BO funds always outperformed VC funds. This raises serious doubts on the

Table 4.2   Pooled sample distribution of private equity funds' PMEs

	PME (MSCI Europe)			BME (JPM European Govt Bond)		
	VC	BO	Total	VC	BO	Total
Liquidated funds						
Average	0.82	0.90	0.86	1.11	1.07	1.09
Median	0.68	0.89	0.80	0.81	1.09	0.99
75th percentile	0.97	1.24	1.10	1.38	1.37	1.38
25th percentile	0.33	0.51	0.42	0.54	0.64	0.58
Std dev.	1.01	0.53	0.81	1.51	0.60	1.14
Value-weighted PME			0.94			1.21
Sample I						
Average	0.98	0.94	0.96	1.14	1.24	1.20
Median	0.75	0.86	0.82	1.06	1.02	1.03
75th percentile	1.17	1.24	1.23	1.44	1.43	1.43
25th percentile	0.40	0.59	0.51	0.66	0.63	0.66
Std dev.	1.15	0.51	0.89	1.02	0.59	1.11
Value-weighted PME			1.04			1.27
Sample II						
Average	1.01	1.06	1.03	1.25	1.06	1.23
Median	0.76	0.92	0.88	0.99	1.13	1.07
75th percentile	1.22	1.35	1.27	1.27	1.42	1.45
25th percentile	0.44	0.61	0.55	0.60	0.77	0.66
Std dev.	1.15	0.70	0.95	1.38	0.74	1.10
Value-weighted PME			1.16			1.30

appropriateness of the IRR for comparing different funds or groups of funds. Hence, for benchmarking the track record of a GP the PME approach will be by far more suitable than an IRR-based approach.

In our empirical analysis, we find PMEs of 0.86 for liquidated funds, 0.96 for sample I and a PME of 1.03, which is larger than one, for the extended sample II. All these results are in accordance with the results of Kaplan and Schoar (2005) for the US market; for instance, they report an average PME of 0.96 when using the S&P500 as the benchmark index. Using the JP Morgan European Government Bond Index as the benchmark index, private equity funds reach an overall superior performance in all subsamples. In all cases the value-weighted average PME is higher than the equally weighted average, indicating that larger funds tend to have a higher PME. (It should be noted, nevertheless, that although the correlation between size of the fund and PME is positive, it is statistically not significant in this sample.)

3.3 Which Factors Determine European Private Equity Fund Returns?

After having presented the results for various performance measures, we shall now raise two much more interesting questions: what are the factors determining these returns and, if such factors can be identified, what are the consequences for the investment strategy of an institutional investor?

According to the theoretical reasoning presented in the introduction and taking into account some findings documented in the literature, we focus on two important return drivers. First, we analyse to what extent returns are triggered by fund inflows into the private equity industry, that is, we address the so-called money-chasing-deals phenomenon. Second, we discuss whether final performance is a matter of luck or rather determined by the skills of the management team of a fund.

3.4 Does Money Inflow into the Private Equity Industry Have an Impact on the Performance?

Because of different research studies, we start with the presumption that the private equity market is not frictionless and perfectly competitive due to specific characteristics: segmentation, stickiness and illiquidity. If this is true, we would expect that money inflows into the private equity industry as well as management skills of the GP can affect the performance of private equity funds.

Gompers and Lerner (2000) show that inflows of capital into venture funds increase the valuation of these funds' new investments. They argue that private equity is an asset class segmented from other asset classes.

Although it is an open question, whether increased valuations are triggered by money pouring into the private equity industry or whether this money flow is triggered by improved expectations with respect to future investment opportunities, and hence by increased valuations, Gompers and Lerner present some evidence that is more consistent with the first hypothesis. They basically argue that there is a limited number of favourable investments in the private equity industry giving way to the money-chasing-deals phenomenon. It is important to note that the soundness of this argument is linked with special features of the private equity asset class, as has been shown in the context of a purely theoretical analysis by Inderst and Müller (2004).

This 'segmentation' argument might be especially important for private equity funds because they are normally not allowed to invest the committed capital in any other asset class as well as in another type of the private equity industry. Even if the GPs were aware of an overvaluation in the industry or in a specific part of the industry, they would hardly be able to redirect their money towards other investment projects.

In this regard, Ljungqvist and Richardson (2003b) point out that capital flows between GPs and LPs (limited partners) tend to be 'sticky', that is, it takes a longer time to adjust the capital invested in the industry to changed expectations or valuations.

In the case of increasing expectations of the investors, due to improved economic prospects, the money inflow rises and the fund management is able to finance more companies. But the question is: how good are these companies and have these investment projects a positive net present value (NPV) or haven't they? If private equity funds invest the additional money in projects with a negative NPV or in projects that have only a positive NPV due to overestimations of future private equity cash flows, the average expected return of the private equity industry decreases.

But if the number of attractive target companies is limited in the short run, the valuation of potential companies increases substantially because there is much more capital supply in the private equity market than demand from attractive portfolio companies. Additionally, Ljungqvist and Richardson (2003b) argue that competition for deals becomes tougher, the more money is pouring into private equity funds, because the number of attractive investment targets is limited in the short run.

Finally, due to *illiquidity* and the absence of a continuous secondary market activity, additional money cannot directly be reflected in increasing asset prices as would be the case in the public market. Hence, the additional money attracted due to improved economic prospects must be absorbed entirely by primary markets, that is, by an adjustment of deal pricing. This effect will be reinforced, if it is taken into account that the largest part of money invested in private equity is allocated through private equity funds.

Our basic idea for setting up an empirical test of the money-chasing-deals phenomenon is to distinguish between the absolute and the relative fund inflow. We assume that the total inflow into the private equity industry is, basically, triggered by economic prospects of the industry as a whole. Hence, the absolute fund inflow in a specific year can be regarded as a measure for the perception of investment opportunities. Under rational expectations these perceptions might turn out to be wrong, but they should not be wrong in any systematic sense. However, as mentioned before, in the short run there might be a mismatch of capital offered and demanded. The impact of such a mismatch would be harder, the more money is directed towards a specific part of the private equity industry and the more segmented the private equity industry is in itself.

A simple example should be given in order to explain this idea. Assume that total fund inflow increases by 10 per cent in a particular year. If positive NPV investment opportunities do not increase by the same size, deal competition might become more intense. However, the impact on the intensity of deal competition might be even more dramatic, if simultaneously the relative size of funds allocated towards VC and BO funds changes significantly. In this situation, deal competition increases substantially for the fund type attracting the larger share of fund inflows, while it may even decrease for the other fund types. This is why we assume that the relative share of funds allocated towards a particular fund type can be regarded as a measure for the intensity of deal competition.

Now, if we assume an overshooting of capital in a specific part of the private equity market, the search costs for private equity funds to get a favourable investment target increase. Additionally, the bargaining power of entrepreneurs increases in such situations. Because of that, ownership shares of the private equity fund decrease and deal valuations on primary markets raise in that particular year. Hence we expect a negative impact on fund returns for funds that are closed in a year with high relative cash inflows. On the contrary, if we imagine a situation with more capital demand than capital supply in a specific part of the industry – while the absolute cash inflow into the industry is high due to increased economic prospects – private equity funds can choose favourable investment targets from many possible candidates. Because of this selection mechanism and because of the lower intensity of deal competition, the bargaining power of private equity funds increases while the valuations for entrepreneurs stay at a normal level. Hence we expect higher returns for private equity funds closed in years with low relative inflows.

In order to check the money-chasing-deals phenomenon, we use the euro-denominated cash inflow into the European private equity industry that is annually published by EVCA. Furthermore we calculate the relative inflow into the venture capital or BO markets, that is the share of capital that is allocated in that particular fund type. For reasons of simplicity we split the sample into just two different fund types, venture funds and buy-out funds. Moreover, we split all the vintage years into years with high and with low absolute inflows as well as with high and low relative inflows, by using the median absolute or relative inflow as the separating parameter.

If the money-chasing-deals phenomenon drives returns, funds closed in periods of (a) high absolute inflows (AI_H) and low relative inflows (RI_H) should have relatively high return measures; (b) high relative inflows (RI_H) as well as low absolute inflows (AI_L) should have lower return measures than others.

According to this hypothesis we can split up the whole sample into four different groups and calculate the average IRR, excess IRR or PME for each group. The results are presented in Table 4.3, where we report the average and median of the return measures as well as the 95 per cent confidence interval (Conf Int) of the average return measures.

Table 4.3 visualizes that funds founded in years with high absolute inflows have statistically higher returns (IRR = 18 per cent) than funds founded in years with low absolute inflows (IRR = 9 per cent). Taking into account that the absolute fund inflows increase from €4.2 billion in 1992 to over €48 billion in 2000, this result corroborates the findings of a previous paper, where we documented that funds with a vintage year in the 1990s have higher returns than funds with a vintage year in the 1980s.

Additionally, we can show that funds founded in periods of high relative inflows tend to have lower IRRs and excess IRRs than funds in times of high inflows. This is also true for the median PME but not for the average PME.

Taking a closer look at the groups of funds in Table 4.3, one can see that funds founded in a phase of high absolute and high relative inflow outperform funds closed in times of low absolute and relative inflows due to the relative strong absolute inflow effect. Concerning the money-chasing-deals phenomenon, the remaining two groups of funds are most interesting. In fact, funds that are founded in periods with high absolute cash inflows (AI_H) as well as low relative cash inflows (RI_L) have the highest returns measured in terms of IRR (20 per cent) and excess IRR (13 per cent). In contrast, funds founded in years with low absolute inflow (AI_L) and high relative inflow (RI_H) have only an average IRR of 4 per cent and a negative excess IRR to the MSCI Europe equity index of −5 per cent. The returns of these two groups are also different in a statistical sense, using a significance level of 1 per cent. These findings strongly corroborate the money-chasing-deals phenomenon.

Table 4.3   *Empirical results for analysing the money-chasing-deals phenomenon (%)*

		RI_L	RI_H	Total
IRR				
AI_L	Average	11.62	3.92	8.83
	Median	9.24	2.79	7.26
	95% Conf Int	(7.83; 15.41)	(1.17; 6.68)	(6.14; 11.51)
AI_H	Average	20.31	16.64	17.89
	Median	14.44	10.99	11.70
	95% Conf Int	(12.80; 27.81)	(9.78; 23.50)	(12.77; 23.01)
Total	Average	14.36	11.69	12.69
	Median	10.80	8.22	9.14
	95% Conf Int	(10.83; 17.89)	(7.24; 16.14)	(9.99; 15.39)
Excess IRR				
AI_L	Average	2.64	−5.12	−0.18
	Median	−0.02	−5.47	−2.44
	95% Conf Int	(−1.41; 6.68)	(−7.99; −2.25)	(−3.02; 2.66)
AI_H	Average	13.26	9.70	10.91
	Median	6.06	2.75	3.30
	95% Conf Int	(5.04; 21.48)	(2.30; 17.10)	(5.37; 16.45)
Total	Average	5.99	3.93	4.45
	Median	1.57	−0.02	0.61
	95% Conf Int	(2.15; 9.83)	(−0.90; 8.75)	(1.52; 7.38)
PME				
AI_L	Average	0.89	0.66	0.81
	Median	0.86	0.68	0.76
	95% Conf Int	(0.77; 1.01)	(0.54; 0.79)	(0.72; 0.90)
AI_H	Average	1.10	1.22	1.18
	Median	0.99	0.82	1.00
	95% Conf Int	(0.87; 1.32)	(0.85; 1.60)	(0.93; 1.44)
Total	Average	0.95	1.01	0.96
	Median	0.86	0.76	0.82
	95% Conf Int	(0.85; 1.06)	(0.77; 1.24)	(0.83; 1.08)

    To sum up: our findings are completely in line with the perception that an overshooting (undershooting) of capital investments in a specific part of the private equity industry is due to some kind of herding behaviour, where investment opportunities on primary markets are systematically overestimated (underestimated) by investors. This fits nicely with another result, namely the sentiment effect, that is, that funds raised in vintage years with high stock market returns have lower returns than funds raised in years with low stock market returns. Hence, putting these findings together one might argue that there is a behavioural explanation for the money-chasing-deals phenomenon in private equity markets. (We showed that the sentiment effect has a statistically significant influence on the performance of European private equity funds. See also Kaserer and Diller, 2004c.)

Of course, private equity investors should be aware of the existence of these phenomena. Hence, a contrarian's investment strategy, that is, investing in private equity funds in times of relative low capital inflows into this specific segment of the private equity industry, might be a superior choice. However, as investment flows in private equity are sticky, such a strategy might be hard to implement. In this case the investor should at least follow an investment strategy that diversifies over different vintage years and within every vintage year over different fund types.

3.5 Do Management Skills Affect the Performance of Private Equity Funds?

From the specific characteristics of the private equity market it follows that skills of the management team could have a more significant impact on fund returns than is the case for funds invested in public market securities. In efficient public markets a great deal of information, public or private, is incorporated in asset prices. Hence, the ultimate outcome of an investment strategy should be almost the same, regardless of whether the investor undertakes informational activities or not. In fact, there is no clear evidence from the mutual fund performance literature that fund returns may be driven by fund managers' skills, such as selection or timing abilities.

We would expect fund management skills to be much more important in private equity funds than in public mutual funds. Knowledge about investment opportunities in the private equity industry may be distributed very unequally and, due to the lack of a secondary market for these assets, it may be a long time before this information is disseminated. Now, if there is a systematic difference in knowledge about private equity investment opportunities among different management teams we would expect that good deals are concentrated in a small number of fund portfolios, that is, the portfolios of the skilled management teams. The first consequence of this idea is that deal returns should have a much more skewed distribution than public stock market prices. In fact, as indicated in Tables 4.1 and 4.2, private equity funds' returns distributions are heavily skewed.

Finally, if skills are unequally distributed at a given point in time it may well be that their distribution is not independent over time. Hence, we would expect that returns of subsequent funds run by the same management team can be correlated. This gives way to the so-called 'persistence phenomenon' in private equity funds' returns. Ljungqvist and Richardson (2003b) and Kaplan and Schoar (2005) documented this for US funds, and Gottschalg et al. (2004) for an international funds sample.

To test the persistence phenomenon in our empirical study for European private equity funds we use different approaches that are known from the mutual fund industry. The assessment of performance persistence is focused on the contingency table methodology of repeated winners and losers. Moreover, financial tests, such as Malkiel's (1995) Z-statistic, Brown and Goetzmann's (1995) odds ratio and Khan and Ruud's (1995) χ^2-statistic, are applied to analyse the robustness of this phenomenon. Concerning the contingency tables methodology, the technique involves comparison of performance rankings in two or more different funds of the same management team. Thus we rank all funds, which have a follow-on fund on the basis of their IRRs. In order to define two subsets of 'winner' (W) and 'loser' (L) portfolios, we use the median of the IRR of all funds to differentiate the funds. The better-performing half of the funds will form the subset of 'winners' and the worst-performing half that of 'losers'. This method is repeated in each sequence. The two-way contingency tables are created by successively comparing the two subperiods. These tables are thus 2×2 matrices reflecting WW funds (winner in both sequences), WL funds (winner in the first sequence and loser in the second), LW funds (loser in the first sequence and winner in the second) and LL funds (loser in both sequences). In Table 4.4, the descriptive results of this methodology are visualized.

Based on results obtained in this table, the existence of the persistence phenomenon may be affirmed because the number of funds maintaining their status as winners or losers is substantially higher than the number of funds that change their status. Fifty-two funds stay in their half while 30 funds change their status. By applying the various statistical methods mentioned above, we find clear evidence for the persistence phenomenon in European private equity funds. Using Malkiel's Z-statistic, Brown and

Table 4.4 Empirical results for analysing the persistence phenomenon

Funds sequence	WW	WL	LW	LL
1–2	11	9	9	10
2–3	7	2	2	6
3–4	5	2	2	5
4–5	2	1	1	1
Following	3	1	1	2
Total	28	15	15	24

Goetzmann's odds ratio and a χ^2-statistic (*p*-value = 0.016) yields statistically significant results on the 5 per cent level for our data sample I. Hence, it seems that better-performing GPs tend to also get a good performance in the follow-on funds. This is also true for poorly performing funds due to the fact that management skill matters. Only 18 per cent of the follow-on funds reach the group of the winner funds in the following sequence, if the proceeding fund was ranked as a loser fund. As has been explained, this result fits nicely into the picture of a sticky and segmented asset class.

The practical consequence of this result can be summarized in the formula 'never change a winning team'. In fact, once it turns out that an investment team is successful, the private equity investor should stick to this team. From this perspective, it makes completely good sense to use the track record of an investment team as an important piece of information in the investment decision process. However, as the track record is almost public information, an investment strategy based on historical performance only cannot be implemented. In fact, funds managed by teams with a successful track record often have the luxury of selecting among investors that will be 'permitted' to invest in the fund. In this respect, the evidence presented here cannot directly be transformed into an investment strategy.

However, there is a more indirect consequence coming out of these results. Once it is accepted that the skills of the management teams are unequally distributed and taking into account that it is very hard to enter into a fund run by a historically successful management team, it becomes evident that identifying the good teams at the very moment when they start to act as GPs is very crucial. Of course, this chapter does not offer any help as to how this selection takes place, but it gives clear support to why team selection is crucial for becoming a successful private equity investor.

4. CONCLUSION AND IMPLICATIONS

In this chapter a comprehensive dataset of European private equity funds provided by TVE was analysed. Starting with calculating the IRR distribution of a sample of mature European private equity funds, we introduced the PME approach, which we defined as a wealth multiple. A PME of 1.2 tells the investor that for every euro that he/she invests in a specific private equity fund he/she needs to invest €1.2 in a public market benchmark in order to generate an identical cash flow stream. Most interestingly, we were able to show that benchmarking on an IRR basis could lead to substantially distorted results.

Moreover, even a ranking of different funds on basis of the IRR could generate a pitfall. Hence, LPs should not benchmark the track record of a

GP on basis of the IRR; they should use instead the PME. For a sample of 200 mature European private equity funds raised in the years 1980 to 2003 we calculated an average IRR of 13 per cent and a PME of about one.

The main focus of this chapter, however, was to give new insights into the determinants of funds' returns. For that purpose we started from the presumption that the private equity asset class is characterized by illiquidity, stickiness and segmentation. It has been argued in theoretical and empirical papers that these characteristics can cause an over- or undershooting of private equity asset prices, at least in the short run. Most importantly, Gompers and Lerner (2000) have shown that venture deal valuations are driven by overall fund inflows into the industry, giving way to the so-called money-chasing-deals phenomenon. We document that funds founded in a phase with high absolute and low relative cash inflows have significantly higher returns than funds founded in periods of low absolute as well as high relative capital inflows. Hence, the money-chasing-deals phenomenon is an important factor in explaining European private equity funds' returns. From a practical perspective, this result has two implications. First, a private equity investor should implement a contrarian investment strategy, in the sense that he/she invests in those fund types that get a relatively small share of total funds invested in the private equity sector. Second, diversifying invested funds over different vintage years as well as different fund types seems to be very important in order to reduce the risk of being exposed to the money-chasing-deal phenomenon.

Apart from the importance of fund flows, the chapter also shows that GPs' skills have a significant impact on fund returns. More precisely, returns of subsequent funds run by the same management team are correlated. So, we present evidence in favour of the persistence phenomenon governing the returns of European private equity funds. These results underline the stickiness and segmentation of this asset class. From a practical perspective it is, however, rather difficult to derive an investment strategy from this result. Although the result is a justification for why track records are very important for inferring the abilities of a management team, it is of little help as this information is almost public. Nevertheless, the result indicates that the selection of a management team is a key success factor for private equity investments.

REFERENCES

Brown, S. and W.N. Goetzmann (1995), 'Performance persistence', *Journal of Finance*, **50**, 679–98.
Gompers, P.A. and J. Lerner (2000), 'Money chasing deals? The impact of fund inflows on private equity valuations', *Journal of Financial Economics*, **55**, 281–325.

Gottschalg, O., L. Phalippou and M. Zollo (2004), 'Performance of private equity funds. Another puzzle?', Working Paper, INSEAD (European Institute of Business Administration).

Inderst, R. and H.M. Müller (2004), 'The effect of capital market characteristics on the value of start-up firms', *Journal of Financial Economics*, **72** (2), 319–56.

Kaplan, S.N. and A. Schoar (2005), 'Private equity performance. Returns, persistence and capital', *Journal of Finance*, **60**, 1791–823.

Kaserer, C. and C. Diller (2004a), 'European private equity funds – a cash flow based performance analysis', CEFS Working Paper, 2004-01, www.cefs.de.

Kaserer, C. and C. Diller (2004b), 'Beyond IRR once more', *Private Equity International*, July/August, 30–38.

Kaserer, C. and C. Diller (2004c), 'What drives cash flow based European private equity returns? Fund inflows, skilled GPs and/or risk?', CEFS Working Paper 2004-02, Center for Entrepreneurial and Financial Studies, www.cefs.de.

Khan, R.N. and A. Ruud (1995), 'Does historical performance predict future performance?', *Financial Analyst Journal*, **51**, 43–52.

Ljungqvist, A. and M. Richardson (2003a), 'The cash flow, return and risk characteristics of private equity', NBER Working Paper 9454, National Bureau of Economic Research, www.nber.org/papers/w9454.

Ljungqvist, A. and M. Richardson (2003b), 'The investment behaviour of private equity fund managers', Stern Working Paper, New York University.

Malkiel, B. (1995), 'Returns from investing in equity mutual funds 1971 to 1991', *Journal of Finance*, **50**, 549–72.

Meyer, T. and T. Weidig (2003), 'Modelling venture capital funds', *Risk Magazine*, October, 27–35.

5. Business angel academies: unleashing the potential for business angel investment

Juan Roure, Rudy Aernoudt and Amparo de San José Riestra

1. INTRODUCTION

Business angels have been revealed as important sources of finance for young and innovative companies. Although their activity remains by large within the private sphere, there are indications that business angels might provide as much as two to five times the capital that venture capital funds invest in early-stage ventures – in the US, about 36,000 companies receive angel finance every year. Widely praised as 'smart' capital, business angels bring their expertise and experience to complement the entrepreneurial team deficiencies.

It is generally accepted that the informal venture capital market is largely undeveloped in Europe as compared to the USA. The European Business Angel Network (EBAN) estimates raise the number of individuals who can be considered to be potential angel investors to 850,000 individuals in Europe and 1,750,000 in the USA. This latent mass of individuals, who fit the profile of business angels but have never invested, are often referred to as 'virgin business angels'. There is evidence that the pool of non-active investors is increasing as compared to investment activity figures. In the USA, and despite the increase in angel groups' membership, 41 per cent of angels in those groups were not active, which represents a steady increase over recent years (Sohl and Sommer, 2003). Anecdotal evidence suggests that the same phenomenon is taking place in Europe. As an example, a majority of Danish business angels in the national network claim to have invested less than 10 per cent of the capital which they had beforehand allocated to investment in unquoted companies.

European policy makers have approached the mobilization of these potential investors from different perspectives. Early policy actions from the European policy level focused on promoting widespread establishment of business angel networks (BANs). More recently, governments have supported a series of schemes to 'leverage' public capital and lower the financial risk of investments. These co-investment instruments broke the departing principle that business angels did not need money. Actions have also multiplied to upgrade communication skills of entrepreneurs looking for finance and making ventures 'investor ready'.

Professionals and experts in the field call for a second generation of business angels better equipped to target reluctant potential investors and entrepreneurs. This second generation of BANs focusing on 'educating' the marketplace (Mason and Harrison, 2002) should also consider the supply side of the market. In this context emerged the idea of a business angel academy or school that could fulfil that role, whereby angels would progress along a learning curve throughout all the phases of the angel investment procedure.

The IESE Business School (Barcelona, Spain) run a pioneer training programme for business angels. Investors would attend 10 sessions of half a day with lectures, workshops and presentations from academics and selected practitioners. More than 50 business angels, potential and active, joined the first intake. Against this background, the aim of this chapter is to identify differences between active and passive business angels, to understand the training needs of business angels and to discern between the training needs of active and passive business angels. Finally we aim at exploring the potential role of nascent business angel academies as an awakening instrument for latent angels and promoters of the informal market.

2. THE ORIGIN OF BUSINESS ANGEL MARKET DEFICIENCIES

Apart from information asymmetries present in all private equity investment, inefficiencies in the functioning of the informal market have been traditionally explained by the existence of an 'information gap' in the market, demand-side problems and contextual factors.

The *information gap* is active at different levels. On the one hand, there is an inadequate flow of good ideas from the demand to the supply side of the market. Investors claim not to have access to enough business proposals or to proposals that match their investment criteria. Entrepreneurs on their side also report having difficulties finding potential investors, who prefer to keep a low public profile concerning their willingness/capability to invest.

On the other hand there is also a *knowledge gap*, reflected in a large number of potential investors and entrepreneurs who have never heard about this type of investment. Entrepreneurs who 'have been told to contact a business angel or business angel network' ask themselves and others 'who are these people?' and 'how can they help us?'.

A further informational element contributing to the inefficiency of the market, that is, the lack of data on investment, exit and return statistics, as well as cases to be analysed and contrasted by researchers and experts, hampers the external assessment of the real opportunity represented by this market and the diffusion of this activity as an investment alternative (Esposito and Prats, 2003).

Demand-side problems have been brought to light, such as the poor quality of the investment proposals received by investors, in particular from first-time entrepreneurs or techno-scientist entrepreneurs, who concentrate on certain parts of the business plan and lack an overall strategic vision. The experience of investors and intermediaries in the field shows that entrepreneurs' lack of knowledge of financial and legal aspects of structuring operations hampers negotiations, making it extremely difficult to agree on acceptable terms and conditions to close an investment operation.

Other elements that influence business angel investment activity, namely taxes, entrepreneurial culture and administrative constraints, have their share of responsibility in the inefficiency of the market.

In response to identified inefficiencies BANs can be considered as the first attempt to create a true mechanism to increase the efficiency of the market and consequent deal flow, which provide the basic 'market infrastructure'. BANs grant a channel of communication between investors and entrepreneurs in order to minimize the cost of the entrepreneur's search for capital and enable investors to examine a larger number of investment opportunities and hence facilitate access to proposals that meet their investment criteria. BANs are also important instruments to bring down the knowledge gap, raising awareness about the market on both sides, between entrepreneurs seeking external capital and potential investors. The networks dedicate increasing efforts to collecting information on the activity of their members. The comparability of results obtained is essential to raise the profile of informal investment as an alternative return seeker activity.

Nevertheless, these attempts to improve the supply of informal venture capital through the establishment of BANs have not always been successful. The relative success of the networks has been both widely endorsed and strongly contended: there is no universal agreement on their effectiveness.

The concentration of efforts to improve framework conditions such as taxes and legal aspects and the promotion of BANs has not been efficient in bringing business angel activity to the desired level. BANs have not as a general rule, with the exception of the 'band of angels', invigorated the syndication phenomenon, which is considered underdeveloped in Europe as compared to the USA. Therefore, further analysis of the informal investment market is deemed indispensable in order to explore new ways to cope with the underdevelopment of the angel market.

3. IN SEARCH OF NEW APPROACHES

The observation of investor attitudes on investment forums and reports on the flow of initial contacts and negotiations are a signal that the lack of competency among investors might be relevant to the underdevelopment of the informal market. A study by Sørheim and Landstrom (2001) classifies investors into four groups, of which only one can be considered to be composed of *classical* business angels. The rest would lack either competency or investment activity. Investor education is a factor inducing a person to move from potential to active investor, and also to create a supportive culture for informal investment. The capacity of investors to assess certain types of ventures also appears to be an issue within the early-stage venture capital market for innovative ventures. In addition, business angels must be able to assess the risk opportunities. This resource is not necessarily acquired alongside management know-how, industry-specific know-how, and financial and networking skills.

In order to increase investment activity of potential investors, and complementary to the BANs, upgrading of investment assessment skills could be a real issue. Freear et al. (1994) propose to look into investment activity as a function of angels' felt level of confidence and competence in their ability to deal intelligently with the 'central mysteries' of venture investment, namely, pricing, structuring and exiting.

Angel investment is a process rather influenced by the personality of the angel. Only a few people have accumulated sufficient experience and capabilities to participate, or even to facilitate, this type of investment. Business angel investment is an activity marked by increasing complexity of businesses and the environments in which they operate. The 'lonely' entrepreneur is more and more a rarity and new high-potential businesses require a broad range of capacities, hence, a team of entrepreneurial individuals often initiates those businesses.

We can argue that an important contributor to this knowledge gap is caused by the lack of an adequate understanding of the investment process, and therefore business angels are less able to take advantage of arising opportunities. While entrepreneurs are often trained to elaborate and present their business plan to investors and are advised on what to expect from investors, the only training for business angels is experience.

Lack of training of investors is a factor whose importance is not unknown to the formal venture capital market. One of the obstacles to the development of the early-stage venture capital market in Europe is the lack of capacity of mainstream venture capitalists to assess the potential of early-stage ventures, in particular, of innovative projects. Most investment analysts hold a finance or economic degree, whereas only one-fifth hold an engineering or other technical degree; however, according to surveys in the venture capital industry, the ideal recruit for this role has a technical degree plus an MBA. Different actions of the European Commission have been addressed to support the long-term recruitment of additional investment managers in order to build within the venture capital industry a lasting capability to appraise and manage those early-stage projects in technologically innovative small and medium-sized enterprises. An evaluation of one of those initiatives concluded that the venture capital industry benefited from a long-term increase in capacity resulting from the engagement and training of new staff.

The angel investment process similarly requires the synchronization of the different components, whose objective is to achieve overall success. From this point of view, the process implies the participation of entrepreneurs, advisers, intermediaries and angels, all with different characteristics and personalities. For capital-seeking companies, the investor is a 'stranger' and for the investor the company is a 'risk'. Hence, an important success factor is the management of the investment process, whereby the entrepreneurial and interpersonal skills are elements as decisive as the provision of capital.

4.   BUSINESS ANGEL EDUCATION: BUILDING INVESTMENT CAPABILITY

According to the above, business angels are (subject to possession of the requisite financial capacity) individuals who have access to investment opportunities, are skilled in discerning the potential of those investment opportunities and eventually capable of managing the complete investment flow to exit. Hence, two resources important to a business angel's investment activity can be identified: *networks*, whether informal or formal, provide the investor with investment opportunities or allow for the sprouting of co-investment operations; and *skills* which will provide the investors with capabilities to assess the risk of investment opportunities and manage the process.

In this context a new area for business schools arises: the business angel academies. The design of such a programme has to recognize the difficulties of narrowing down the profile of investors, their individuality and their tendency to operate beyond official programmes. It can be argued that teaching business angels might have some similarities with

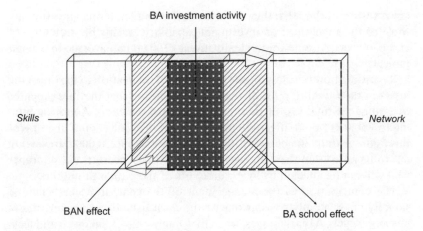

Figure 5.1   Role of business angel schools and BAN in the market

teaching entrepreneurship, and hence the teaching should offer a combination of theory and practical applications that provides students with the basis for their decisions. Along the same lines, informal investment theory should help to understand better how to create wealth. As can be seen from Figure 5.1, a business angel academy should enable investors to increase their activity for a given deal flow. It should not only mobilize virgin angels and increase the activity of the existing angels, but should be a tool for promoting syndication. Especially in Europe, greater syndication is a must in order to cope with the smaller equity gap problem, as the average amount invested by a business angel in a project does not enable the investee to survive until the company is ready receive formal venture capital.

5.   THE TARGET OF BUSINESS ANGEL ACADEMIES

The results of the survey show that individuals attending to the Business Angel Academy (BAA), including active and passive business angels, have similar characteristics to those reflected in other research, namely, they are male, between 35 and 55 years old, with an entrepreneurial past, financial capacity to invest and the desire to be involved in the venture (see Hindle and Rushworth (2001) for a summary of previous descriptive studies on business angels).

The wealth and risk profile of the angels enrolled in the programme also reflects similar results to existing research. Business angels have on average €470,000 available for investment. The median is very similar and only very few investors declare that they are able to allocate €2 million to investments. Most of the angels have an investment capability varying between €60,000 and €300,000. Angels would ideally invest €100,000 on average in a single project.

Regarding how business angels approach risk in relation to the impact of losses in their wealth, most of the investors declare that they are prepared to assume the total loss of their investments (65 per cent). A loss amounting to €50,000 would affect the family wealth of 5 per cent of the angels; this figure rises to 36 per cent if the loss amounts to €150,000. However, it has to be noted that there are wealthier (or riskier) investors (23 per cent), who will not be affected by losing amounts of more than €1 million.

The contribution to the management of the company, whether occasionally or on a daily basis, is one of the most valuable characteristics of business angels. At early stages, when they mainly invest, financial and technology assets are not a guarantee for success: new companies lack managerial skills and need help on the marketability of the product. The strong commitment of angels is also present in the size of the stakes they subscribe. Although not seeking control, their stake might depend on either the perception of the risk of the project or the market. Respondents to the survey reported their preference to be involved with the firm as coaches or advisers, and they expressed willingness to dedicate an average of 26 hours per month:

Coach	50%
Member of the board	35%
Minority shareholder (no involvement)	10%
Variable, depending on the investment	5%

Business angels might, as widely reported in research, have time to dedicate themselves to the new venture because their accumulated wealth and their professional capacity is largely proved, and they therefore do not feel the pressure that (younger) professionals or entrepreneurs feel in earlier stages of their career. But business angels are rarely retired or idle. As few as 8 per cent work part-time and they are involved (on average) with more than three institutions, boards or foundations.

Regardless of their investment experience, participants in the school programme have significant entrepreneurial experience. As many as 69 per cent have started a new business at least once and most of them can be deemed to be serial entrepreneurs, since the average number of enterprises created by each investor is three (mean: two). Nearly half of angels (46 per cent) currently own an enterprise (the questionnaire does not specify whether they were initial entrepreneurs on that business or whether they bought in at a later stage). Hence, many of these angels are already in the third career phase, and have been through the corporate career phase, the entrepreneurial learning phase, and the integrated investment career phase; the understanding of their career choices may prove helpful in directing efforts to locate and attract potential and existing informal investors. Certainly these informal investors are 'entrepreneurial learners' who continue to develop their entrepreneurial skills throughout their career, resulting in a valuable competence that they can share as informal investors with less-experienced entrepreneurs.

Traditional sectors are the most frequently cited as a source of professional experience, namely, manufacturing (the region of Catalonia – where the IESE is based – has a strong tradition in textile manufacturing), financial services, construction and distribution (either retail or wholesale). Since experience determines future investment of business angels, who normally invest in the sectors they know best, it seems that business angels are not a panacea when dealing with technology-driven new ventures. In fact, during the working sessions held with attendees at the school they expressed a certain suspicion of high-tech ventures.

This is consistent with the approach of angels across Europe. For instance, British business angels invest only 30 per cent of the total amount in the high-tech sector, while manufacturing and services represent 64 per cent. Also NEBIB, the Dutch BAN, reports that most angels in the Netherlands 'have earned their money' in enterprises that offer a mixture of services and sales. The view that 'venture-building' skills are widely applicable to any number of industry settings is confirmed by research carried out on German business angels, who no matter what previous experience they have (only 40 per cent had previous experience in the sector they invested) show a clear preference for diversification to technology sectors instead of remaining in the sector where they gathered that experience. For instance, German business angels with experience in the trade sector dedicated 52 per cent of their investments to information technology, 21 per cent to life sciences and 20 per cent to the services sector.

As mentioned above, the participants at the school were not only virgin or latent business angels. On the contrary, the majority of them (69 per cent) reported that they already had experience as a business angel. Many of these are already experienced or serial business angels, since the average number of investments carried out by them is two. Some of them were closing their first investment deal at the time of joining the school (shown in Figure 5.2 as 'in process').

Angels mention returns and the need to pursue personal challenge as the main reasons to invest. Equally, business angels are aware of the opportunities offered by their personal and business networks and want to realize

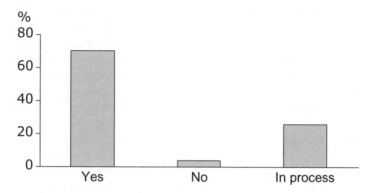

Figure 5.2   Business angel experience of school participants

these opportunities using their own and their families' wealth. The social component, although it does not appear among the most important reasons to invest, is also present, together with the perception of social responsibility to coach the next generation of entrepreneurs.

Business angels can also act as 'love money' investors by financing the ventures of family members and friends. Nevertheless, this criterion ranks among the lowest they take into account. Finally, business angels are not tax-driven investors, although they take into consideration the fiscal framework of investment; in this survey, fiscal incentives appear as one of the least important reasons for investment.

In common with other surveys carried out in Europe, we observe that returns are always among the top three reasons to invest, together with personal challenge or satisfaction and the willingness to pass on knowledge to new entrepreneurs. In general, taxes do not play a relevant role. However, low rates of capital gains seem to be the main factor to encourage investment, in the same way as high rates are the main discouraging factor.

Differences seem to exist between European angels in terms of stage of the venture in which they invest. Spanish business angels are much more prone to invest in the seed stage than their British counterparts and resemble German business angels more in this respect (we assume that the pre-start-up seed category in the German survey is included in the seed category for the Spanish survey) (see Table 5.1). The similar distribution of amounts invested in the UK and Spain, does not explain or lead to an understanding of the different stage investment pattern exposed.

Active and passive business angels possess, as seen before, similar characteristics. However, there might be certain differences that contribute to the lack of investment activity among virgin angels. The identification of

Table 5.1   Investment stage pattern (%)

Investment stage	Spain	UK	Germany
Seed	61	8	25
Pre-start-up seed			38
Start-up	17	25	45
Other early		32	
Development	22	28	16

these differences is essential to the attempt to mobilize passive capital, that is, the diagnosis should be made prior to the treatment.

6.   POTENTIAL BUSINESS ANGELS

As many as 30 per cent of participants in the school have no investment experience – they are *virgin* business angels – but they are conscious of their angel potential and take steps to turn themselves into active angels. Their main reason for not investing is the 'lack of information on opportunities arising and poor knowledge of the sectors of opportunities received' (75 per cent), followed by 'not knowing adequately the investment procedure' (37.5 per cent) and, third, 'lack of attractive projects' (25 per cent) and 'high risk' (25 per cent). Only one of them claimed illiquidity as a reason for not investing.

Investment capacity of passive angels is slightly lower than for active angels. Passive angels would dedicate €100,000 (€300,000 for active angels) to investment, investing €70,000 (€150,000 for active angels) per project, which reflects a higher risk aversion, exacerbated by their lack of experience in the market. The proportion of enterprise owners is higher among active angels as is the case for entrepreneurs (80 per cent of active angels against 37 per cent of passive angels).

Motivations of passive business angels to invest are 'expected returns' followed by 'social benefit' and 'support to the new generation of entrepreneurs' (see Figure 5.3). While active angels share the main reason, return, this group ranks personal challenge and taking advantage of its social network as the second and third reasons. It seems that passive angels also attribute higher importance to social contribution, either in the form of direct knowledge transmission and support to young entrepreneurs or through direct and indirect benefits to society of fostering entrepreneurship.

Passive and active angels have a range of similar and different expectations from attending the school (see Table 5.2). Given the investment experience of

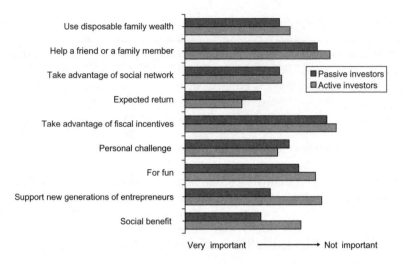

Figure 5.3   Motivations to invest (scale from zero to five)

Table 5.2   Expectations of attending the school

	Importance ranking		Importance ranking
Active angels		**Passive angels**	
New business valuation	1	Research, identification and evaluation of opportunities	1
Research, identification and evaluation of opportunities	2	Relations with other investors and exchange of experiences	2
Growth strategies	3	Growth strategies	3
Business plan analysis	3	Business plan analysis	4
Team management	3	New business valuation	4
Deal negotiation	3	Deal negotiation	4
Relations with other investors and exchange of experiences	3	Divestment process	5
Divestment process	4	Team management	5
Financial forecast analysis	5	Legal aspects of investment	5
MBO–MBI	5	MBO–MBI	6
Legal aspects of investment	5	Financial forecast analysis	6

active angels (two operations on average) their interest in the school moves forward into more advanced stages of the investment process.

Despite placing considerable importance on the research, identification and evaluation of opportunities, active angels would like to improve their business valuation skills, a problem with which many passive angels have not been confronted, since they did not invest due to lack of information on opportunities arising and sectors. The results also show that active angels are more aware of the relevance of the exit procedure than virgin angels; again this is less relevant for those who have never reached that stage. In different working sessions organized with angels, many of them pointed out that planning the exit strategy while discussing the deal was essential. For both groups, the focus on financial forecast analysis is the least important aspect of the teaching to be provided by the school. Management buy-out (MBO) and management buy-in (MBI) investments are also of little interest (at least in the framework of business angel investment and the school).

The informal venture capital market is apparently considered to be inefficient by both groups of angels, passive and active, since their difficulty in finding projects is similar. Relationship with other investors is also essential for both groups. Throughout all the work sessions organized by the school, it was clear that angels, especially those with less experience, considered it essential to establish a platform that allows for the exchange of experiences, provides access to the advice of experts or more sophisticated investors and facilitates the occurrence of syndication. When it comes to the matter of establishing arenas where investors and entrepreneurs can meet, it seems obvious that the kind of BANs that offer only matchmaking services would not be sufficient to push them into investing. Generating opportunities for experienced business angels to act as mentors and catalysts for the other groups of investors and to establish varying social encounters in order to further foster interrelationships between the different types of investors could be very beneficial.

7.   CONCLUSION AND IMPLICATIONS

We have shown that angels, whether active or passive, feel the need to improve their investment skills. The survey carried out among participants at the BAA provides strong support for the proposition that there are potentially different training lacunae between active and passive investors.

Virgin business angels are affected by this lack of knowledge in the first and decisive stages of investment: the recognition and evaluation of opportunities. Therefore, they are hampered in carrying the process further. Active angels value primarily training in the area of new business valuation. Indeed, it is reasonable to think that virgin angels have not been able to overcome initial difficulties of the investment process, the identification of opportunities, while active angels recognize their main difficulty once they are involved in the investment.

Passive business angels would initially invest in the lower amount range of investments, which reflects their higher risk perception. At the same time, they demand more comprehensive services from the business angel networks they join. Co-investment with other angels is also one of the reasons that would trigger their first investment.

Those angels, active and passive, who acknowledge the existence of training lacunae, are prepared to follow academic-type courses. The large majority of student angels surveyed put most value on in-depth study of topics, organization of working groups to analyse cases and a broad framework for exchange of experiences. Despite time constraints, angels value continuous education and are willing to follow structured and longer programmes than the majority of those available in the market.

The programme available at the Angel Academy provides an entry route for virgin angels. There is a significant learning curve associated with appraising and managing investment opportunities, and angel syndication provides a means for virgin angels to gain experience while taking less risk than if investing alone. As a consequence of some features of the programme – namely, the long academic period, frequent working sessions with rotating small groups, and required regular attendance of participants – the first iteration of the programme resulted in a very cohesive group and the discussion of several co-investment opportunities.

As a result of the findings of this study, we propose an innovative alternative targeting the reduction of information asymmetries from the supply side through the provision of investment education to business angels. The training of business angels would improve their knowledge of the investment process, hence reducing risk and stimulating investment. Furthermore, the different actors in the market should be coordinated to lower inefficiencies. In such a framework the development of an equity-seeking mindset, the so-called 'equity culture' between entrepreneurs, can be fulfilled by the education system and the public bodies which the entrepreneur addresses in the first place when looking for help in establishing a business.

Educational organizations, such as business schools offering structured programmes with a combination of academics and practitioners, are best placed to provide the tools that potential angels need to complete their first investment and start progressing within the learning curve. European institutions could play an active role by integrating the BAA concept into their benchmarking exercise.

REFERENCES

Espasito, A. and Prats, M.J. (2004), 'La dinámica de la información en el mercado informal de capital riesgo', *Iniciativa Emprendedora*, **42**, IESE-Deusto, Barcelona, 3–16.
Freer, J., Sohl, J.E. and Wetzel, W.E. Jr (1994), 'Angels and non-angels: are there differences?', *Journal of Business Venturing*, **9** (2), 109–23.
Hindle, K.G. and Rushworth, S. (2001), 'The demography of investor heaven: international research on the attitudes, behavior and characteristics of business angels', in M. Whincop (ed.), *Bridging the Entrepreneurial Financing Gap: Linking Governance with Regulatory Policy*, Aldershot, UK: Ashgate, pp. 10–37.
Mason, C. and Harrison, R.T. (2002), 'Barriers to investment in the informal venture capital sector', *Entrepreneurship and Regional Development*, **14**, 271–88.
Sohl, J.E. and Sommer (2003), 'The private equity market in the USA: lessons from volatility', *Venture Capital Journal*, **5** (1), 29–46.
Sørheim, R. and Landstrom, H. (2001), 'Informal investors in Norway – a categorization with policy implications', *Entrepreneurship and Regional Development*, **13**, 351–70.

PART II

The Entrepreneur's Perspective on the Role of
Private Equity

6. The motivation of entrepreneurs towards private equity financing: a laddering approach

Gabriele Morandin, Massimo Bergami and Richard P. Bagozzi

1. INTRODUCTION

The purpose of this chapter is to contribute to our understanding of entrepreneurs' motivations to engage in private equity financing. This topic has important theoretical, methodological and practical implications that we shall elaborate upon below. In addition, the subject is timely in the light of debate on the consequences of the rate of growth of firms and on the governance model of the firm. Guiso et al. (2004) claim: 'local financial development has a positive and statistically significant effect on firm's growth'. At the same time, other authors confirm the importance of entrepreneurial skill and motivation to venture growth, giving important implications in this regard.

The topic of private equity financing has traditionally been studied from financial or business strategy perspectives, but analysis is generally lacking with respect to the reasons for or explanations of private equity financing that considers cognitive, motivational and cultural forces on decision making when the opportunities offered by advanced financial markets are absent. This is also a relevant theme from the point of view of political economy, as the limited knowledge of institutional investors and their modality of intervention represent the main obstacles for the use of innovative instruments able to support the firm's growth and economic development. In addition to these factors, affective or emotional responses could induce mistrust and counterproductive reactions among entrepreneurs having to make joint decisions. The firm's refusal of operators that are not strictly familiar turns in most cases into a refusal of the managerial culture and of the opportunities of growth offered by markets.

An important step needed to remove these stereotypes resides in entrepreneurs' motivation towards private equity financing, which this chapter will study, thereby encouraging an empirically grounded cognitive and motivational prospective in entrepreneurial studies.

2. MAIN ARGUMENTS

2.1 Means–End Chains and Cognitive Schemas

Empirical studies on motivation have traditionally relied on long checklists of general motives. But the motives on such checklists are often too general, overlap, and neglect relationships between motives (for example, the possibility that motive x leads to motive y which promotes risk taking). Moreover, the theoretical basis for the motives on such checklists is often lacking, and the fit to a particular decision context is typically strained. A more specific approach is needed to uncover motives that decision makers actually have and how these motives guide, influence, or interfere with actual decision making.

An approach that recently has attracted scholarly attention is 'means–end chain theory' (MEC theory; Bagozzi and Dabholkar, 2000), a model first proposed and formalized in marketing but recently applied with success to relevant individual decision making in the psychology literature as well (Bagozzi et al., 2003).

The basic assumption of the model defines motives not so much with reference to internal stimuli *per se*, but in terms of goals. In the original version of MEC theory, 'means' are construed as instruments, procedures, or activities in which people engage, while 'ends' are valued states of being; a means–end chain is a model that seeks to explain how a decision to choose a product or activity facilities the achievement of desired end-states; in other words, some motivations (*means*) are functional in achieving goals (*ends*) that occur at different and deeper levels of an individual's motivational structure.

This theory seems particularly suited for the present study, because entrepreneurs choose to share their equity with an institutional fund for the purpose of reaching goals that are not solely connected to financial motives. In addition, MEC theory can be used to discover entrepreneurs' mental images and frameworks about institutional investors, people towards whom entrepreneurs are often diffident yet dependent.

MEC theory supposes that a decision maker's individual knowledge is hierarchically organized such that concrete thoughts are linked to more abstract thoughts in paths that proceed from means to focal ends. The knowledge structure of a person with regard to a situation is represented by *cognitive schemas*, defined as 'learned, internalized patterns of thought-feeling that mediate both the interpretation of on-going experience and the reconstruction of memories' and in particular influence decisions (D'Andrade, 1992). The basic units of cognitive schemas consist of two kinds. The first is 'declarative knowledge', which consists in individual motives to which the focal end is linked directly or indirectly through chains of motives. Declarative knowledge, which is connected to knowledge of a focal issue, refers to specific concepts and characteristics that serve as a basis for decision making. MECs, starting from concrete decision criteria or motives and reaching to more abstract criteria, constitute the building blocks of individual decision makers' cognitive schemas. Connections among declarative knowledge units (that is, motives) are termed 'procedural knowledge', and function in thinking processes like if–then propositions (for example, if lower-level motive x is satisfied, then it will bring higher-order motive y into play as a more proximal determinant of a decision).

MECs in the form of interconnected motives and hierarchically organized, represent modalities that people use implicitly in decision making. A person's knowledge structure and motives (that is, organized declarative and procedural knowledge) become the basis for decision making. In this way schemas provide motivational force, in fact schemas 'have the potential of instigating action – that is, they can function as goals' (D'Andrade, 1992, p. 29). It should be noted that declarative and procedural knowledge occur in cognitive schemas where conscious, deliberative decision making occurs. For cognitive schemas that represent associative, non-conscious memory networks, the knowledge so entailed is neither declarative nor procedural but can harbour some minimal levels of awareness or sense of experience.

In other words, to realize why someone behaves the way they do it is not enough to know the discourses, objects and events to which they have been exposed; these dimensions have to be integrated into the psychic structures that assimilate those things and turn them into a basis for decision making and meaningful action.

On the basis of Bagozzi et al., (2003) framework, we propose that any focal goal can be related to reasons for acting and depicted through a three-tiered hierarchy:

> One's focal goal can be considered at the centre of the hierarchy and answers the question, *What* is it for which I strive? Subordinate goals constitute the means for achieving the focal goal and answer the question, *How* can I achieve that for which I strive? Subordinate goals have been treated as concrete actions in what some researchers call the *program level* in control theory. At the top of the hierarchy are superordinate motives, which answer the question, *Why* do I want to achieve that for which I strive?. (p. 917).

The motives in a hierarchical schema are connected through means–ends linkages at each level of the hierarchy, and at the superordinate level in particular many motives typically exist in complex relationships. It is the superordinate level that we focus upon in this study.

MEC theory can also be called a 'model of meaning'. A basic assumption is that the full meaning of a concept is given by the other concepts with which it is associated. Thus, a single concept such as 'innovation' or a price of '$100' has little or no explicative meaning by itself. To understand what 'innovation' or '$100' means to a person, we must identify the other concepts to which it is connected. For example, the meaning of innovation (for a firm) is determined by its association with other concepts like investments, research and development, new products and revenue. The network of perceived connections to the 'innovation' concept determine its fuller meaning for that person. Using procedures such as laddering, which will be introduced in the next subsection, these linkages reveal the true meaning of each important concept a person has.

In summary, the advantage of discerning cognitive schemas is that it leads to testable hypotheses concerning how new information is represented in memory, as well as the ability to trace the inferential processes involved in judgement and choice for existing sets of information, and to suggest target thoughts and inferences for change by means of persuasive communication.

Moreover, treating goal schemas as motives or, more precisely, as 'having motivational force', allows us to overcome limitations in traditional motivational studies (D'Andrade, 1992). First, the question of identifying which reasons are associated with which behaviours can be answered by analysing MEC linkages. Second, the fallacy of relying on a list of general and universal motives is avoided in the sense that it is clear that there is no one list of motives and that there are at least as many types of master motives as there are types of goal schemas. Third, situational variance becomes more explicable: schemas are context dependent and thus yield a deeper, more valid comprehension of specific situations. Finally, one of the most important advantages of considering reasons for acting or decision making as schemas with embedded goals is that it not only connects cognition and decision making to behaviour, but it also shows how goals are patterned at different levels of abstractness and thus become pathways for influencing decision makers, as will become clearer below.

2.2   Laddering Technique

Scholars of MEC theory have developed a methodological approach, called 'laddering' (Reynolds and Gutman, 1988), to uncover the hierarchical structure of the superordinate motives that provide reasons for pursuing a particular focal goal.

The original laddering technique depended upon an in-depth, one-on-one interviewing technique that was used to develop an understanding of how people translate the perceived attributes of products into meaningful associations with respect to one's self as a consumer and to develop an understanding of the motivational and cognitive processes that induce people to purchase a product or adopt a service. Laddering involves use of a tailored interviewing format consisting primarily of a series of directed probes, typified by the 'Why is that important to you?' question, with the express goal of determining sets of linkages between the key perceptual elements across the range of attributes, consequences and values that constitute a cognitive schema for products or services. The general outline of such schemas consists of a perceived attributes → felt psychosocial consequences → experienced value hierarchy of interlinked thoughts.

Following Bagozzi and Dabholkar (2000) and more recently Bagozzi et al. (2003), our adaptation of the laddering technique involves use of ideas proposed by S. Toulmin on argumentation and rhetoric. According to Toulmin, arguments can be considered as a series of claims that an arguer provides to support an argument; each claim, in turn, can be challenged on the basis of its justification; justifications, in turn, rest on evidence and can also be challenged or explained. We adapted this framework to discover chains of reasons and reasoning for analysing.

The laddering interview can be summarized as follows. First, respondents are asked to list their personal reasons for choosing a focal goal. After listing their reasons, respondents are asked to return to the first reason they gave and then to express why that reason was important to them. Next, respondents are asked to explain further why the explanation was so important to them. Finally, the above procedure for providing justifications and explanations is repeated for the remaining reasons on the original lists one at a time until deeper levels of justification are expressed.

In our case, we first asked entrepreneurs to list up to five reasons why they would allow institutional investors to participate in the firm's equity decisions. Then for each reason listed, one at a time, entrepreneurs were asked to answer two sequences of questions concerning why the motivation was important for the person, in the sense of explaining their reasons, and then giving a justification for each of their explanations. Box 6.1 presents the questionnaire format.

BOX 6.1   ELICITATION OF MOTIVES QUESTIONNAIRE

We would like you to express your personal reasons for allowing institutional investors to participate in the firm's equity.

For the questions below, please follow this sequence: *1.* List five reasons you have for wanting to allow institutional investors to participate in the firm's equity and place these in the boxes in column #1 under REASONS. *2.* Then take your first reason and think of why this is important to you. Please your answer in the box adjacent to your first reason in column #2. *3.* After answering why your first reason is important, think about why the answer given is, in turn, important, and put your response in the box in column #3. *4.* Repeat Steps 2 and 3 for each remaining reason in column #1. We have place numbers in the upper left corners of each box to remind you of the sequence to follow.

REASONS	WHY – 1	WHY – 2
Reasons for allowing institutional investors to sparticipate in the firm's equity	Why is it important?	Why is it important?
1	6	11
2	7	12
3	8	13
4	9	14
5	10	15

The data derived from the laddering procedure permit the application of a content analysis (illustrated below) so as to develop an understanding of how consumers translate their motives or reasons for acting into meaningful associations with respect to personal goals and values. The aim is to disclose key decision criteria and linkages among the most important decision criteria that decision makers implicitly follow in their decision making and which influence their actual choices and action. This technique used to identify cognitive schema can be employed to identify motivational goals; the basic idea is that cognitive schemas function as goals, and so have motivational force.

The laddering technique was applied to a sample of 91 entrepreneurs from the Emilia Romagna region of Italy who were in a position to consider private equity financing. The sample was selected in such a way as to obtain an equal geographical distribution across the region. The interest in 'local' financial development is also an important theme for its impact on the economic success of an economic area (Guiso et al., 2004).

2.3 Motives and the Cognitive Map

The content analysis of all ladders given by the 91 entrepreneurs was carried out by two independent judges and produced nearly 906 distinct reasons in total (with a mean of 9.96 motives per entrepreneur) and 520 linkages among motives (mean of 5.71). Because the responses obtained in a laddering interview are typically rather idiosyncratic, it is necessary to classify the raw data into a limited number of response categories (Reynolds and Gutman, 1988). In our case this meant assigning responses of entrepreneurs in the laddering interview to a small, yet comprehensive, set of goal categories. The final encryption based on a semantic analysis of all reasons and using the recommended coding procedure from the literature identified 37 unique motivations, which in turn can be classified into three general categories, as presented in Table 6.1. One category is linked to market and business dimensions, including aspects associated with the competitive environment and opportunities following the entry of the investor into an equity relationship; a second category is linked to firm variables, including managerial and organizational efficiency issues; and the third dimension is linked to the entrepreneur, *per se*, with aspects reflecting personal goals and one's family. It is important to point out that the dividing line between reasons belonging to the first two categories is a fine one, and some reasons (for example, firm growth) could possibly have been assigned to either category. In other words, the boundary between firm motives and market/business motives is fuzzy. This is not a limitation of the procedure or findings because the categorization procedure is done merely for presentation purposes.

Table 6.1   Three main categories and relative frequencies of motives mentioned by entrepreneurs

Firm motives	Frequency	Market and business motives	Frequency	Personal motives	Frequency
Productive capacity	16	Acquisition	23	Personal growth	14
Managerial competencies	61	Strategic alliances	25	Disagreement among partners	13
Firm growth	67	Competitiveness	64	Liquidate investments	16
Organizational efficiency	41	Share risk	11	Personal satisfaction	22
Sales	15	Environmental factors	23	Way of life	7
Products range	13	Corporate image	34	Succession	22
Ideas	16	Leadership	17	Tradition	11
Innovation	36	Network	10	Family connections	21
Investments	33	New capital	57	Vision	14
Lower costs	15	New markets	19		
Shakedown	16	New partners	24		
Financial solidity	38	Bargaining power	28		
Corporate survivorship	23	Quoted on the stock exchange	7		
		Market share	31		
		Corporate market value	3		

The frequencies observed suggest something about the content of entrepreneurs' cognitive schemas. The motivations with higher frequencies belong to the categories of firm and market; firm growth, competitiveness and managerial competencies are in fact the most frequently mentioned motivations, each with frequencies above 60; but note also that new capital and organizational efficiency have high frequencies as well. Regarding personal motives of entrepreneurs, we observe that lower frequencies occur; the highest personal values occur for personal satisfaction and succession, where both were mentioned 22 times.

Now that the salient goals for motivating institutional investors to participate in the firm's equity have been identified, we next examine the relationships among these goals. In this way we can discover the hierarchical relations among the goals, and by organizing goals from the concrete to the abstract, we hope to gain insight into the entrepreneurs' cognitive schemas related to their decision making with respect to private equity financing. The first step is to construct an 'implication matrix', which contains the observed links among different motives. The implication matrix is a square matrix whose elements reflect how often goal *i* leads to goal *j*. The matrix (available from the authors upon request) shows as only a small proportion of how all possible relations between goals are actually manifested. There are a total of 1332 possible relations, but only 295 cells contain direct paths of one incidence or more, yielding a proportion of about 22 per cent of all possible paths. The 91 respondents mentioned a total of 590 direct linkages among goals.

In order to arrange the goals in a meaningful way we computed an index of the level of abstractness for each goal as the ratio of in-degrees to the sum of in-degrees plus out-degrees. In-degrees show how often a motive is the object or the end of a relation, whereas out-degrees indicate how often a motive is a source or origin. The abstractness ratio measures the proportion of times a motive serves as a destination in a cognitive schema, as opposed to a source. The assumption is that the more abstract the motive, the more likely it will be an end, where the range of values is from 0.158 (for succession), the most concrete goal, to 0.800 (for the sales reason) which is the most abstract goal.

The information provided in the implication matrix can be simplified by developing a visual map of the main 'goal chains', which are aggregated sequences of goals that are formed over both respondents and specific goals within categories.

To construct a goal map, it is necessary to select a cutoff value for linkages among goals. A cutoff was chosen based on linkages occurring four or more times following the above criteria, following procedures indicated in the literature. It allows us to account for 26 per cent of all relations between goals made by entrepreneurs using only 2 per cent of all possible cells in the implication matrix and only 9 per cent of the cells that contain a non-zero entry.

With this information, it is possible to construct a mental map for entrepreneurial motivation (Figure 6.1). This map is derived directly from the implication matrix but only selecting linkages mentioned four or more times. Arrows in Figure 6.1 reveal the direction of linkages among motivations, while numbers placed alongside represent the frequency with which the relation has been observed in the sample. The vertical dimension of the map represents the degree of abstractness; motivations with lower degrees of abstractness are at the bottom, while motivations with higher degrees of abstractness are placed above these.

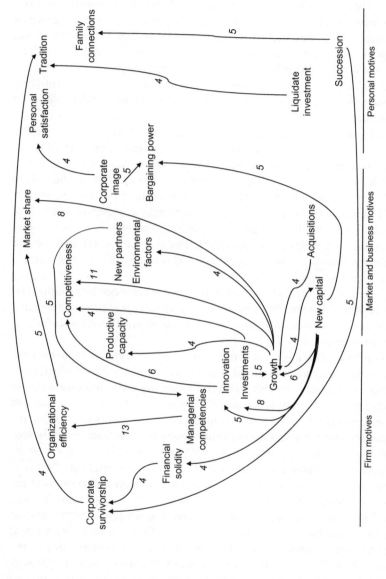

Figure 6.1   The entrepreneur motivational map showing key motives and their linkages and arranged hierarchically according to degree of abstractness

By analysing jointly the frequency with which motivations appear and the cognitive map as a whole, it is possible to conclude that entrepreneurs give more attention to firm consequences. In particular, firm growth, besides being cited most frequently by entrepreneurs (67 citations), also shows the highest number of links with other reasons or motives (both as a destination or source), displaying a high degree of centrality in entrepreneurs' cognitive schemas. Located among motivations at the bottom of the map, growth is a source or influence of such important goals as competitiveness and market share.

The link from growth to competitiveness, in particular, is important for three reasons: First, it is the second most frequently mentioned link in the schema with 11; second, competitiveness was also cited frequently by entrepreneurs (64 times); and third, competitiveness is the motive with the highest centrality value (centrality is an index measuring the transformative role of motives and is computed with a formula discussed below).

The relation of growth to market share is also relevant thanks to its observed frequency of occurrence (8), but also because it shows the linking directly of a concrete motivation with an abstract one (research shows that abstract motives are the most proximal determinants of decisions, yet must be 'reached' or influenced with change strategies aimed at concrete motives).

Note that the most abstract goals in Figure 6.1 are market share, personal satisfaction, tradition and family connections. This would be expected to be the strongest predictors of actual decision making but themselves would be vulnerable to influence by targeting their direct antecedents. For example, market share is directly dependent on organizational efficiency and growth. These, in turn, may be influenced by persuasive messages targeted at their lower-level antecedents. Another channel of influence particularly interesting is the one that connects managerial competence with organizational efficiency. Managerial competencies, located in the centre of the map, is a relevant node thanks to its relatively high frequency cited by entrepreneurs (61). Moreover, the observed strength with which managerial competencies connects with organizational efficiency (13) suggests its importance.

It may be concluded that the most meaningful links among motives begin with firm criteria and end with motivations directly connected to such market and business opportunities in the competitive environment as competitiveness and market share. With respect to motives concerning entrepreneur characteristics, two links are noteworthy. One goes from succession, the most concrete motivation in the map, to corporate survivorship and in turn to the motive of tradition; the other goes from succession to family connections. The resort to private equity financing with this finality

Table 6.2   Prominence indices derived from goal structure

	Centrality	Prestige
Productive capacity	0.014	0.008
Managerial competencies	0.050	0.021
Competitiveness	0.056	0.035
Firm growth	0.055	0.017
Organizational efficiency	0.039	0.016
Environmental factors	0.023	0.014
Corporate image	0.032	0.020
Innovation	0.030	0.012
Investments	0.030	0.011
Liquidate investment	0.010	0.003
New capital	0.043	0.008
New partners	0.022	0.013
Bargaining power	0.029	0.017
Market share	0.028	0.020
Personal satisfaction	0.018	0.014
Financial solidity	0.035	0.017
Corporate survivorship	0.022	0.014
Succession	0.014	0.002
Tradition	0.011	0.007
Family connections	0.018	0.011

could therefore be seen as an attempt to overcome all too familiar dynamics that risk slowing down, complicating or even compromising the delicate process of succession. Finally it is important to observe that as all motivations are widely linked among themselves in complex patterns, many other motives and their interconnections play potential roles in decision making as well.

To gain an indication of the importance of the different goals for the sample of respondents, it is informative to examine the property of goal prominence from the literature on network analysis. There are two important measures of prominence, where prominence might be conceived as an indication of the degree or magnitude that a goal serves as a source or object in the goal hierarchy. More formally, 'centrality' is a measure of how frequently a particular goal is involved in relationships with other goals and indicates how frequently a particular motive is involved in linkages with other motives. The second measure of prominence is called 'prestige', and measures the extent to which a particular motive is the target of other motives. Table 6.2 shows the results for the prominence indices applied to the goals that are in the cognitive map.

With respect to centrality, competitiveness is the most important goal based on linkages, in the sense that it is the source of the most linkages. Firm growth and managerial competencies are also central goals. Liquidate investment and tradition are somewhat less central. Also, with respect to prestige, competitiveness is the most important object of other goals, followed by managerial competencies and corporate image. These results reinforce the previous analysis and interpretation of the cognitive map and give more importance to market and business reasons than to material and immaterial reasons.

3.   CONCLUSION AND IMPLICATIONS

This chapter presents a novel approach to private equity financing by entrepreneurs, as it combines ideas from behavioural research (that is, psychology and organization studies) with ideas from business (that is, finance and economics). The research also employs a unique methodology (a second-generation MEC theory and laddering technique to a rare data set of entrepreneurs and their judgements.

The main contribution of this study is to apply the new MEC theory and the laddering technique to decisions to engage in private equity financing by entrepreneurs. The threefold category of decision criteria we identified are somewhat similar to those found in previous studies for venture growth, but we deepen the foundation of what specifically are the constituents of the categories and how they function, as expressed in cognitive schemas. We thus provide a more detailed, yet holistic, framework for how decisions are made.

The identification of a motivational map (cognitive schema) represents a starting point for studying the relation among motivations and other consequences of decisions by entrepreneurs to share the equity of the firm. To validate any cognitive schema, the motives and linkages among motives can be used as independent variables in multiple regressions to predict decisions, attitudes and other outcomes.

For future research, the results of this study suggest criteria (that is, specific motives and linkages between motives, where the latter constitute if–then propositions) to include on survey questionnaires in order to verify the decision criteria discovered in this research. On the practical side, this study contributes to our understanding of why entrepreneurs (and firms) make the decisions they do, bringing out the entrepreneurs' desire for firm growth, so as to maintain the competitiveness of their firms in the market and improving market share or the viability of a market niche. In addition, this research potentially provides practical suggestions to institutional investors and policy makers with regard to the bases of decision making that entrepreneurs exhibit.

Finally, whereas personal traits and inclinations can be modified only with great effort and difficulty, considerable research findings suggest that patterns of thought and errors arising from them are often more amenable to learning. Thus, not only does our research offer the possibility of new conceptual tools useful in entrepreneurship research, but it also suggests routes to effective interventions for encouraging entrepreneurs' training and education.

In sum, we believe that we have taken a big step in reducing the asymmetry in information between local entrepreneurs and institutional funds, encouraging at the same time the development of forms of social capital (that is, trust, see Guiso et al., 2004) among these relevant actors.

REFERENCES

Bagozzi, R.P., Bergami, M. and Leone, L. (2003), 'Hierarchical representation of motives in goal setting', *Journal of Applied Psychology*, **88** (5), 915–43.

Bagozzi, R.P. and Dabholkar, P.A. (2000), 'Discursive psychology: an alternative conceptual foundation to means–end chain theory', *Psychology & Marketing*, **17** (7), 535–86.

D'Andrade, R.G. and Strauss, S. (eds) (1992), *Human Motives and Cultural Models*, Cambridge: Cambridge University Press.

Guiso, L., Sapienza, P. and Zingales, L. (2004), 'The role of social capital in financial development', *American Economic Review*, **94** (3), 526–56.

Reynolds, T.J. and Gutman, J. (1988), 'Laddering theory, method, analysis and interpretation', *Journal of Advertising Research*, **28**, 11–31.

Toulmin, S. (1958), *The Uses of Argument*, Cambridge: Cambridge University Press.

7. What factors determine the use of venture capital? Evidence from the Irish software sector

Teresa Hogan and Elaine Hutson

1. INTRODUCTION

New technology-based firms (NTBFs) are major conduits for translating scientific knowledge into commercial products and processes, and play a vital role in the development and diffusion of innovation. (NTBFs are defined as independent ventures less than 25 years old that supply a product or service based on the exploitation of an invention or technological innovation.)

In order for such firms to thrive, it is critical that they receive appropriate finance at start-up, through to commercialization and growth. Academics and practitioners agree that venture capital is the most appropriate source of finance for NTBFs. NTBFs tend to satisfy the requirements of classic venture capital, which is a medium-term source of funding used to finance investment activities such as research and development, targeted at new or young firms with the potential to grow and expand. Software NTBFs fit the profile of preferred venture capitalist investments in that they have significant potential for rapid value creation, being in new, expanding markets, with products that are protectable by patent and copyright, and with founders who are generally keen to see their businesses grow.

In this chapter, we report the findings of a novel research programme into the venture capital financing of high-technology small businesses in Ireland. Based on a survey of 110 privately held indigenous software companies, of which 54 are venture capital backed and 56 are not, we investigate what factors affect the use of venture capital in NTBFs. Four of our eight explanatory variables relate to the traits of the lead founder: education to degree level and to post-graduate level, prior start-up experience, and management experience in the software sector. A fifth human capital variable is the size of the founding team. We also examine the impact of product lead times, start-up costs, and founders' willingness to relinquish control.

2.   THE SURVEY

We sent questionnaires to the population of Irish indigenous software product companies, which comprised 257 firms in May 2002. The number of valid returns was 117, giving an impressive response rate of just under 46 per cent. In 82 per cent of firms the lead founder and chief executive officer completed the questionnaire. (The remaining 18 per cent were also founders and held other key positions in the company.) The number of venture and non-venture capital-backed firms in the study is similar: 56 of the 110 (51 per cent) firms for which data are available had not received venture capital backing, and 54 (49 per cent) were funded by venture capitalists. (Seven firms were excluded on the basis that they provided insufficient information on whether or not they had received venture capital funding.) This proportion of the sample that is venture capital backed is rather high even among NTBFs, confirming that 'software products' is a sector that attracts considerable venture capital interest. Table 7.1 provides summary information on the sources of finance for the 96 firms that provided detailed funding information. The figures for the full sample show a 50/50 divide between internal and external sources. A mere 4 per cent of financing is sourced from banks, and the remaining outside finance is equity (39 per cent) and grants (7 per cent). Venture capital comprises an average of 28 per cent of financing for the sample firms, with the largest representation among firms 2–4 years old.

Table 7.1   Sources of finance for current investment requirements

Stage	Internal sources (%)			External sources			
	Savings	Other internal	Total internal	Bank loans	Venture capital	Other external	Total external
Start-up (< 2 yrs)	43.0	29.5	72.5	0.0	13.0	14.5	27.5
Commercialization (2–4 yrs)	10.0	22.0	32.0	3.0	38.0	27.0	68.0
Growth (5–10 yrs)	9.5	46.0	55.5	6.5	28.0	10.0	44.5
Mature (> 10 yrs)	10.0	66.0	76.0	5.0	11.0	8.0	24.0
Full sample	14.0	36.0	50.0	4.0	28.0	18.0	50.0

3.   WHAT DETERMINES THE FOUNDER'S DECISION TO USE VENTURE CAPITAL?

3.1   Work Experience

The prior industry experience of the lead entrepreneur is critical in the venture capital selection process, and the received wisdom is that venture capitalists like to back strong teams. Studies show that venture capitalists tend to favour firms founded by people with relevant experience in the industry (Muzyka et al., 1996). The entrepreneurship literature also stresses the benefits of an experienced management team for the survival and growth of new firms, and such firms should be attractive to potential financiers. Prior experience should also give entrepreneurs a greater knowledge and familiarity in dealing with potential providers of finance. We separate experience into two different variables: experience in a previous start-up, and management experience in the software sector.

We find, rather surprisingly, that venture capital backing is more likely when the founder has not previously been involved in a start-up. Twenty-seven out of 56 (48 per cent) non-venture capital-backed firm founders were previously involved in a start-up, whereas only 21 out of 54 (39 per cent) venture capital-backed founders had start-up experience. This difference, however, is not statistically significant.

One possible explanation for this finding is that founders previously involved in start-ups have considerable wealth to bring to the new business, earned perhaps from accumulated retained earnings or from the proceeds of a trade sale. If the 'serial' founder brings more wealth to the new venture, this may reduce the need for external funding. To examine this possibility, we tested whether 'serial' founders had greater initial start-up capital than firms with founders who had no start-up experience. The median start-up cost for both was in the band €63,500 to €127,000, and statistical tests confirm that this difference is not significant.

Figure 7.1 depicts our findings on the relation between prior management experience in the software sector and venture capital backing. The figure shows clearly that in each 'years of experience' category there is very little difference between the proportions that are and are not venture capital backed. This runs contrary to the received wisdom in the venture capital industry. It is also inconsistent with the evidence on venture capital selection criteria, in which the lead entrepreneur's industry experience is considered critical. Similar to the findings about prior start-up experience, this suggests that the factors considered important prerequisites for venture capital support are not the same as those affecting the founder's demand for venture capital.

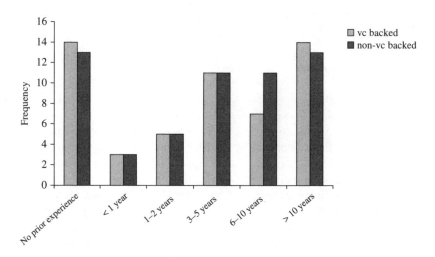

Figure 7.1   Management experience in the software industry

3.2   Size of the Founding Team

The venture capital literature is unanimous in its support for venture teams. There is a strong intuitive argument for the benefits of multi-founder businesses, in that 'many hands make light work'. Because starting a business is a complex process, a founding team should increase the new venture's chances of survival and subsequent growth, in which case teams may have a greater propensity to seek outside finance in order to support the anticipated growth.

Similar to the experience variables, there appears to be no difference in team size between firms that are venture capital backed and those that are not. Figure 7.2 depicts this relation. Eleven out of 26 (42 per cent) of the single founder firms are venture capital backed, compared to 43 out of 84 (51 per cent) firms founded by teams of two or more founders. The difference between these proportions is not statistically significant. Can teams having greater combined financial resources, and therefore not needing external finance, explain the insignificance of the team size variable? Dividing the sample into small (less than €63,500 initial capital) and large firms (greater than €63,500 initial capital), we can conclude that team size is positively related to initial capital. The median team size for firms starting with less than €63,500 is two, and for those with more than €63,500, the median team size is three. This difference is highly significant, confirming that the larger the team, the greater the capital founders bring with them.

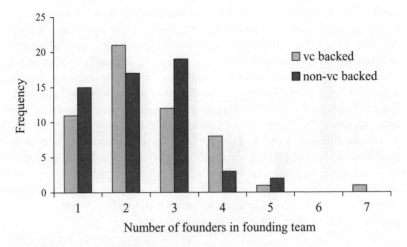

Figure 7.2   Size of the founding team

3.3 Educational Background

A considerable body of academic research has consistently found that the educational background of founders is not important in the venture capital selection process. In contrast, education is often used as a potential explanatory variable in research on the performance of small firms, and it is well established that education to degree level has a positive effect on survival, profitability and growth. This significantly positive relation, however, does not hold for education beyond degree level. How might educational background affect founders' demand for funds? In so far as founders with degrees are keen to see their businesses grow, it is likely that such firms will require external funding to support this growth. Growth firms tend to be more highly geared than non-growth firms, and external equity is more likely to feature as a source of finance in fast-growth firms.

Consistent with prior research on firm performance, we find no relation between education beyond degree level and venture capital backing. On first-degree qualifications, however, our findings are strongly supportive of a positive relation between educational attainment and venture capital backing. Only three out of 54 sample firms (6 per cent) with venture capital backing had founders who were not educated to degree level, compared with 15 out of 56 founders (27 per cent) in firms without venture capital backing. This difference is highly statistically significant.

While education may be considered unimportant by venture capitalists, it is certainly an important demand-side determinant of venture capital backing. Why might this be the case? Apart from the argument that degree holders are keener to see their businesses grow, superior education may equip entrepreneurs to negotiate effectively with potential financiers (Oakey, 1984). We suggest two reasons why the founder's educational qualifications may improve his or her chance of successfully applying for venture capital. First, entrepreneurship research has shown that the founder's degree qualifications are associated with lower levels of NTBF failure. Highly educated founders may therefore be seen by venture capitalists as lower risk propositions, in which case they may well find it easier to obtain finance. Second, a degree may be considered to be a critical qualification for founders in high-technology businesses. Because advanced technical skills in electronic/software engineering or programming would probably be a prerequisite for founders in the software industry, a degree may have a 'certification effect'; that is, it provides an important measure of suitability for starting a high-technology business.

3.4   Product Lead Time and Start-up Costs

NTBFs differ from the general population of start-ups in that they are characterized by an intensive period of research and development early in their life cycle. There is evidence that the longer the product lead time, the more likely it is that the NTBF will require external funding. NTBFs in the biotechnology sector, for example, are more likely to require venture capital funding than firms in other high-technology industries because they face longer product lead times and take longer to reach break-even point than their counterparts in the electronic and software sectors (Oakey, 1995).

Figure 7.3 depicts the sample firms by lead time. There appears to be little difference in lead times for venture versus non-venture capital-backed firms, and statistical testing confirms that the difference is not significant. Venture capital-backed firms do, however, have higher start-up costs. The median non-venture capital-backed firm had start-up costs in the lowest range of less than €63,500, while the median venture capital-backed firm is in the range €127,000 to €317,000. Figure 7.4 shows that the difference in start-up costs between venture and non-venture capital-backed firms is most dramatic in the smallest cost category (less than €63,500), and the largest (greater than €1,270,000). Of the 49 firms in the lowest start-up cost category, 63 per cent are not venture capital backed; and of the 10 firms with start-up costs greater than €1,270 000, only two are not venture capital backed.

So while start-up costs are positively related to venture capital finance, this is not due to longer product lead times requiring greater external finance. In fact, we find no relation at all between product lead time and external financing. This can be seen from Figure 7.5, which plots mean and median product lead times against the start-up cost categories. The figure clearly

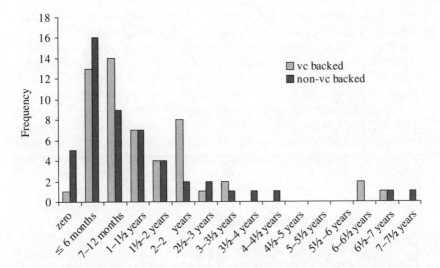

Figure 7.3   Product lead time

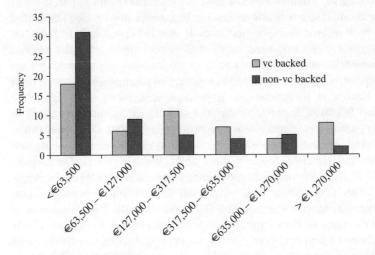

Figure 7.4   Start-up costs

shows very little variability in lead times across the start-up cost categories. The median product lead time for small firms (with start-up costs of less than €63,500) of 13.5 months is slightly higher than that for larger firms (10 months), but this difference is not significant. Our research indicates that Oakey's (1984) finding that firms with longer product lead times need more

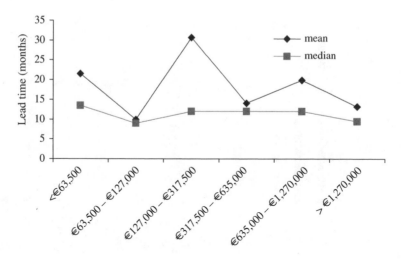

Figure 7.5   Product lead times versus start-up costs

access to external finance does not hold in the software product sector. The software product sector is unique among high-technology industries in that it has very short lead times – a median of 12 months in our sample. Software firms may not, therefore, need substantial outside finance for the product development phase of their life cycle.

If the positive relation between venture capital funding and start-up costs cannot be traced to differences in product lead times, how can it be explained? It is well understood that the venture capital industry tends to avoid very small new firms. Gompers and Lerner (2003) argue that this is because venture capitalists are under pressure to raise large fund pools, and small investments are not worth their while. We test this explanation by assessing whether the proportion of venture capital-backed firms is greater among larger firms (those with more than €63,500 initial capital) versus small firms (those with less than €63,500 initial capital). The proportion of large firms using venture capital – 36/61 or 59 per cent – is significantly greater than the proportion of small venture capital recipients (18/48 or 38 per cent). Assuming that this fact is well known among high-technology entrepreneurs, small-time founders would be unlikely to seek venture capital.

3.5   The Willingness of Founders to Cede Control

One of the strongest stylized facts from the entrepreneurship literature is that independence is the primary objective of owner-managers in small firms (LeCornu et al., 1996). The unwillingness of owner-managers to relinquish

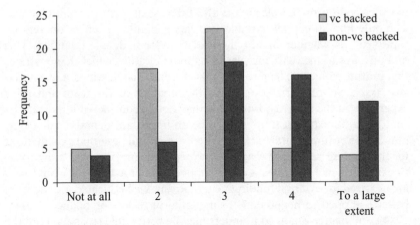

Figure 7.6   Willingness of founders to cede control

control will, of course, predispose them to self-funding. To obtain venture capital support, owner-managers must give up a substantial equity stake; typically 50 per cent. If owner-managers accept venture capital finance, they must be willing to give up a considerable degree of decision-making flexibility and managerial freedom. The variable *control* measures the extent to which the founders expressed a preference to maintain ownership of 50 per cent or more of the shares of their companies, and a higher value for the response implies less willingness to relinquish control. Figure 7.6, which presents our findings on this issue, demonstrates a very strong relation between the founders' willingness to relinquish control and venture capital backing.

Figure 7.6 reports the response to the statement '[prefer to] retain a majority stake-holding (50 per cent or more) in the business for the founders', separated into venture and non-venture capital-backed firms. Survey participants were asked to respond on a scale from 1 to 5, where 1 is 'not at all' and 5 is 'to a large extent', implying that the higher the response number, the less willing is the respondent to relinquish control of the business.

The median response to this question is 3.0 for venture capital-backed firms, and this is significantly lower than the median 3.5 for those not venture capital backed. Founders who are willing to cede ownership are clearly more likely to use venture capital funding.

4.   CONCLUSION AND IMPLICATIONS

Using survey data for 110 Irish indigenous software product firms, of which 54 are venture capital backed and 56 are not, we examined the extent to which eight firm-specific factors affect the use of venture capital finance. The only human capital variable that has a significant effect on venture capital use is whether or not the lead founder is degree qualified. This finding is at variance with the venture capital literature, which demonstrates that venture capitalists tend to downplay formal qualifications, and emphasize 'track record' variables such as the strength of the team and prior experience in the industry. Education may not be considered important by venture capitalists, but it appears to be an important demand-side determinant of venture capital backing. There are several potential explanations for this finding. Owner-managers educated to degree level are more likely to expand their businesses, and to support this growth there would be a greater need for external funding. Alternatively, well-educated founders are better equipped to negotiate with potential providers of finance (Oakey, 1984), and degree qualified founders may be better able to understand the trade-offs involved in accepting venture capital finance.

Our other human capital variables – prior start-up experience, management experience in the software sector, and size of the founding team – are not significant determinants of venture capital backing. This is a rather curious result because it appears to be contrary to the findings in the venture capital appraisal literature. While venture capitalists claim to favour firms with strong, experienced teams, it would appear that many experienced teams eschew venture capitalists. Our findings question whether venture capitalists actually follow their own advice in appraising management teams, or whether they rely on more subjective approaches to appraisal – like 'gut instinct'.

We find a significantly positive relation between start-up costs and venture capital backing. But longer product lead times do not imply that venture capital use is more likely, suggesting that product lead time is not the main driver of start-up costs in software product companies. This is contrary to the evidence from the NTBF literature that the longer the product lead time, the greater the initial capital required, and the more likely it is that the firm will require external funding. However, prior studies compared lead times across industries, whereas we look at the issue within the software sector. Our findings that lead time is very short, and that external financing is at its maximum for 2–4 year-old firms – when it comprises 68 per cent of total funding – suggest that the greatest demand for finance in software product firms is during the commercialization phase.

The most significant explanatory variable in our modelling is the willingness of the founders to relinquish control of their businesses. Consistent with one of the best-understood stylized facts from the entrepreneurship literature, a substantial proportion of Irish indigenous software firm founders view independence and control as critical motivators. If independence is the most important factor behind NTBF financing decisions, perhaps we can conclude that founders bring in venture capital partners reluctantly, or at least after very carefully weighing up the costs and benefits of venture capital finance. Our findings also suggest that founders may initiate ventures with others in order to reduce the requirement for external funding. We find that the bigger firms – those with start-up capital of more than €63,500 – had been started with significantly larger teams than the start-ups with less than €63,500. Not only does starting a business with a team increase access to 'internal' resources at start-up. Because software development is a labour- rather than a capital-intensive activity, the founding team, allowing the reduction or postponement of labour expense, can undertake it. Software firm founders may thus have considerably more financial flexibility than their counterparts in other NTBF sectors.

It is clear that the factors affecting the demand for venture capital financing differ from those affecting the supply. Venture capitalists minimize the risk of their portfolio of investments by choosing firms that they perceive are likely to prosper and grow. This manifests as client firms with teams of founders who have strong experience in the industry and in starting small businesses. However, it is clear from our findings that many NTBFs that may well meet venture capitalists' requirements do not make themselves available for venture capital funding. The implication for investors in venture capital funds is that they do not have access to the full population of young, high-technology firms.

REFERENCES

Bolton Committee Report (1971), *Report of the Committee of Inquiry on Small Firms*, Cmnd. 4811, London: HMSO.

Gompers, P. and Lerner, J. (2003), 'Equity financing', in, Z.J. Acs and D.B. Audretsch (eds), *Handbook of Entrepreneurship Research*, Boston, MA: Kluwer Academic Publishers, pp. 267–98.

LeCornu, M.R., McMahon, R.G.P., Forsaith, D.M. and Stanger, A.M.J. (1996), 'The small firm financial objective function', *Journal of Small Business Management*, July, 1–14.

Muzyka, D., Birley, S. and Leleux, B. (1996), 'Trade-offs in the investment decisions of European venture capitalists', *Journal of Business Venturing*, **11** (4), 273–87.

Oakey, R.P. (1984), *High Technology Small Firms*, London: Frances Pinter.

Oakey, R.P. (1995), *High-technology New Firms: Variable Barriers to Growth*, London: Paul Chapman.

8. Cross-border venture capitalists' support for the internationalization of new software ventures

Markus M. Mäkelä and Markku V.J. Maula*

1. INTRODUCTION

Many of the fastest-growing born global ventures in small open economies such as Finland, Sweden and Israel have attracted cross-border venture capitalists (CBVCs) to support their internationalization. In this chapter, we show how CBVCs can provide substantial internationalization support for portfolio companies that need to expand across national borders from a country with limited domestic markets. However, we also show why these potential benefits do not always materialize. Despite venture capitalists' increasing importance to rapidly internationalizing new ventures, little research has examined the role of foreign venture capitalists in supporting the internationalization process of their portfolio companies. In this chapter, we outline roles that CBVCs (defined as venture capitalists that manage their investment from a country foreign to the investee venture) play in internationalizing new software ventures that have their primary markets in a foreign country.

We used the grounded theory methodology to obtain our results from the analysis of internationalization processes of seven software companies. We collected the data primarily by interviews of entrepreneurs and venture capitalists and secondarily by browsing the companies' web pages, related press releases, www news services, newspapers and other documents. Our results speak to the importance of planning investor strategy according to the internationalization strategy and selecting optimally positioned CBVCs to support internationalization. If CBVCs are located in a venture's target market of internationalization, they can be valuable by legitimizing the unknown new venture in that market, providing contacts, and organizing knowledge. However, foreign investors tend to drive portfolio companies towards areas in their close vicinity, even if this location is not optimal for the venture. Therefore, investor selection can have a significant, long-lasting impact on the development of the portfolio company.

2. TWO THEORETICAL PERSPECTIVES ON INTERNATIONALIZATION SUPPORT

In this section, we introduce two theoretical perspectives on international support which our research draws from and to which our research contributes to: the network perspective and the institutionalization perspective of internationalization.

The *network perspective* on internationalization examines the effects of companies' network affiliations – such as investors – on internationalization decisions. The basis of this approach is in the resource dependence view, which posits that firms importantly depend on resources that are controlled outside the firm. To gain access to resources and to, for instance, sell goods, firms need to establish relationships. According to the network perspective, the force driving internationalization is the desire to use and develop resources so as to serve the long-term economic objectives of firms, including ensuring survival. This model describes industrial markets as networks of relationships that span firms. Internationalization is taken to mean the building of new relationships and restructuring or exiting old ones so that the firm can associate with partners located in foreign markets. Networks can help internationalizing firms by exposing them to opportunities and learning, and enabling the benefits of pooling resources.

Research on social capital that discusses network-related issues is of relevance to our discussion here. Researchers have found that the personal contact networks of founders and employees are the basis for developing a young firm's exchange relationships. Managers' external ties promote conformity between firms and can thus be used to obtain information about what behaviour is acceptable in foreign markets.

Research on growing ventures has shown that such ventures exploit their managers' social capital in forming alliances. This pattern may be considered within the domain of internationalization as well. Prior research has argued that direct personal contacts in foreign markets could be used to obtain advice, identify new business opportunities, obtain assistance in foreign negotiations, and open doors in new markets. It has also been shown in prior research that social capital promotes the acquisition and creation of knowledge. Taken together, social capital is considered highly relevant when explaining the internationalization behaviour of firms.

By participating in ventures' management and providing various resources, venture capitalists provide important non-financial value added to their portfolio ventures. Anecdotal viewpoints hold that they also provide valuable internationalization support. However, there is not much wisdom in a written format on what roles are played by cross-border and local venture capital investors in investment syndicates.

The *institutionalization perspective* pertains to a process in which an actor transforms so as to be similar to its counterparts within its context. The property of similarity is customarily called 'isomorphism' in this literature, and the process of becoming similar is referred to as 'isomorphic change'. In the domain of our discussion here, isomorphic change refers to companies becoming similar with their peer companies that operate in the same geographical market.

Why are some organizations and organizational forms more successful than others? Institutional theorists attempt to explain this via the concept of 'legitimacy'. Things that are generally perceived or assumed by people or organizations as being suitable or appropriate in the surrounding social context are 'legitimate'. Legitimacy is a driver of organizations' performance. At the inter-organizational level of analysis, conformational pressures emerging from company networks define what is socially appropriate conduct and thus influence companies' actions. Prior research in the intersection of internationalization and institutional theory has addressed, for instance, the pressures exerted on a strategic business unit regarding its choice of entry mode. Research has shown that the institutional environment of the host country and the internal institutional environment of the parent organization affect the entry mode of a strategic business unit via an isomorphic process.

Internationalizing firms typically face a number of obstacles and challenges that they need to overcome to achieve legitimacy. Obstacles that companies face at the beginning of conducting business abroad are called 'liabilities of foreignness'. At times when CBVCs support internationalization, they effectively decrease the liabilities of foreignness that their portfolio companies face.

3. INTERNATIONALIZATION PROCESS CASES

In our research, 49 interviews, observations, and several secondary sources were used to collect data on the role of CBVCs in the internationalization of seven ventures. The interviews were semistructured so that the conversation could develop freely according to the answers of the respondents, and to allow in-depth inquiry into the nature of the subject issues. All entrepreneurial respondents were members of the venture's management team, often chief executive officers (CEOs). Nearly all venture capitalist respondents were the representatives of their employers in the venture's governance. In some cases, several venture capitalists from the same firm were interviewed for the same portfolio firm. The interviews were carried out in Summer 2002. In our data analysis, we followed the grounded theory methodology.

Internationalization patterns and the most important business regions of the case companies are illustrated in Table 8.1. To connect these data with venture capital investments, the table also describes rounds of venture capital investments, including their dates and an important detail about the investors – the geographic area from which they have managed their investment.

4. CROSS-BORDER INVESTORS AND NEW VENTURE INTERNATIONALIZATION

The key finding that emerged from the data was that the existence of cross-border investors is likely to lead to a conforming process in which the investee firm, to an extent, becomes more similar to its peers in the geographic areas from which the investor manages the investment or other areas in which the investor has a physical presence. This represents an isomorphic process. Investors can exert pressure to conform to an isomorphic form, and cross-border investors have much power in exerting pressure on ventures.

Several of the CBVCs in the data have exercised some form of persuasion or coercion. Often, this occurred in decisions pertaining to where the company should internationalize its operations. In ventures that internationalized to locations that had been planned as target markets, significant benefits were obtained from cross-border investors. Significant conformational pressure was present in Antares, Betelgeuse and Pollux, while Altair, Capella, Rigel and Procyon experienced less pressure. The subsections below detail how the effects in question were divided into positive and negative effects for the ventures.

4.1 Positive Effects of Isomorphism

At least for ventures that start their business in locations other than their most important market, there can be notable benefits stemming from the participation of CBVCs that local venture capitalists typically cannot provide. A comment from a Finnish entrepreneur illustrates the need for cross-border investors that is often present in firms that are about to start internationalizing to their most important markets:

Table 8.1   *Description of investment rounds and internationalization*
patterns of investee firms

Name and founding date[a]	Rounds[b]	Internationalization	
		Entry modes	Level of foreign sales[c] and key countries
Altair 1997	#1: Summer 1999; Finland, Finland #2: Fall 2000; Northern Europe, Finland, Finland, Central Europe, four other firms	Export sales from Helsinki HQ. Collaborative agreements with major partners that operate globally. In 2001, there was a sales function in the UK, operating in another firm's premises. Technical training is given to foreign firms	About 20%. Developed countries in Asia, Eastern Europe, and Scandinavia
Antares 2000	#1: Winter 2000; Finland, Finland, about 10 very minor investors #2: Summer 2000; Finland, California, Finland, about 20 minor investors	Export sales. Foreign sales personnel without office. Collaborative agreements. Offices: Germany (2000); US East Coast (2000; has been running a low profile since 2001); Quebec (2000; closed down in 2001)	50–75%. UK, Germany, Italy
Betelgeuse 1999	#1: Winter 2001; Finland #2: Fall 2001; Finland, Finland, Northern Europe	Export sales. Foreign sales without offices. Offices: Netherlands (2000); Germany (2000); UK (2001); Sweden (2002)	About 50%. Germany, Sweden, UK
Capella 1997	#1: Summer 2000; Finland #2: Summer 2001; Finland, UK	Export sales. Foreign sales personnel without office. Collaborative agreements in Spain, Portugal, and Germany, and with multinational corporations. Sales offices: Singapore (2001); UK (2001)	50–75%. UK, Hong Kong, Singapore
Pollux (HQ on US East Coast since Winter 2001) 1997	#1: Summer 1999; Central Europe #2: Summer 2000; Central Europe, US East Coast #3: Winter 2002; US East Coast, US West Coast	Export sales. Collaborative agreements. Offices abroad: sales office in the UK (1999); European marketing operations office in Germany (1999; this office no longer has any regular personnel, but exists); office and HQ in US East Coast (2000); sales office in Sweden (2002)	Over 90%. USA, Southeast Asia, Denmark
Procyon 1999	#1: Spring 2000; Finland, Finland,	Export sales from the HQ. Collaboration with large	About 100%. UK,

Table 8.1   (continued)

Name and founding date[a]	Rounds[b]	Internationalization	
		Entry modes	Level of foreign sales[c] and key countries
	additionally an angel from Finland #2: September 2001; Finland, Finland, Northern Europe	partners. Recent collaborative agreements in Spain (2002) and Austria (2002)	Switzerland, Italy
Rigel (HQ on US West Coast since 1999) 1992	#1: Fall 1997; Finland, Finland #2: Fall 2000; California, London, Munich, Finland, seven other investors	Export sales. Foreign sales without offices. Distribution agreement to China (2001); 17 offices, the most important being Netherlands (1995); US West Coast (1998); US East Coast (2000); France (2000); Japan (2000)	About 80%. Key customers are global

Notes:
a. All names are pseudonyms. The firms' headquarters (HQ) were located in Finland – two exceptions are marked.
b. The column presents the dates and for each investor firm, the location from where it managed its investment.
c. Estimated. Foreign sales refers here to sales outside the country of *founding* of the firm.

> Finnish venture capitalists should consider what value added they can bring to an internationalizing company – especially to one whose markets are abroad and there is a multicultural personnel with language proficiency . . . if a Finnish investor lacks competence related to internationalization, a foreign investor will be a respectable option [to be taken on board].

First, according to our findings, cross-border investors bring, at the minimum, enhanced endorsement for their portfolio companies. In our data, all cross-border investors brought endorsement. The results imply that this endorsement is most significant in the geographical vicinity of the investor. The investors' fit with the target market was associated with the strength of the endorsement. To summarize, it appears that all CBVCs provide some form of endorsement to a venture (potentially excluding some investors with a generally adverse reputation; such investors are not present in our data).

Second, cross-border investors can significantly lower the liabilities of foreignness experienced by the venture in the new market by providing contacts and market and other knowledge, that is, foreign organizing knowledge. The positive effects are likely to occur when the investor firm has a close match with the venture's target internationalization market, either operating in that market or originating from there. An instance of the latter case is a US venture capital firm that manages a European investment from a European office and can help the portfolio firm internationalize to the US market. An investor stationed in the correct market can also induce the aforementioned benefits, adding to the endorsement benefits discussed earlier. That is, the investor can drive an institutionalizing process in which the venture achieves yet a greater level of legitimacy in the focal market. Table 8.2 (below) illustrates that the help of CBVCs was typically viewed as being very beneficial in the cases, and that this help appears to be pivotal in decreasing the liabilities of foreignness experienced in internationalizing ventures.

Third, our data support the intuitive notion that cross-border investors are likely to possess far better information on the business environment in their location than the venture that is about to internationalize there. Venture capitalists' knowledge of legal issues is a special domain that several interview respondents raised as an important contribution. We thus integrate provision of legal knowledge into our proposition on foreign organizing knowledge provided by CBVCs.

Fourth, foreign market contacts – a form of international social capital – represent an important resource that was often present in the respondents' accounts: it appears that the existence of a CBVC in the selected target internationalization market is associated with the investee firm having better social capital, including social capital connecting them to potential new investors. Here, our results support prior literature in the observation that obtaining more financiers is one of the key activities of venture capitalists. The appearance of a venture as more attractive to investors operating in a certain location is also a phenomenon that may result from the conformity resulting from the isomorphic processes.

To summarize, venture capitalists may have several positive influences for venture internationalization: they can increase the venture's legitimacy by providing endorsement, knowledge of the business and legal environment, and international social capital. These effects will decrease the liabilities of foreignness faced by the venture in the new market.

Events in the cases illustrate how cross-border investors have provided benefits to portfolio companies when they operate in the correct target markets or originate from them. For instance, in the case of Antares, an American investor with fit on the US market that was not in this case expected to provide as much active contribution as the Finnish investors actively influenced and helped the firm in planning for its US office, providing market knowledge and important contacts. In this process, pressure was involved. According to the early views of the entrepreneurial team, only limited help would have been needed because the team possessed substantial prior experience in international business. Yet, Antares gained significant benefits.

In the cases of Capella and Rigel, the cross-border investors had a good fit with the target internationalization markets and could have exerted strong influence on internationalization, but have nevertheless not done so. In Capella, the US investor's presence brought about major endorsement benefits, and Rigel has enjoyed endorsement as well. In Rigel, a part of the cross-border investors' inactivity may be due to the fact that the venture has a very experienced management and may thus need less advice. The management, however, are slightly of the view that their venture capitalists do not have the best possible expertise in internationalization. This could potentially be a factor that makes investors less willing to exert conformational pressure.

It appears that the good fit of the cross-border investor with a market that has been recognized as a target market is important in enabling the realization of endorsement's best benefits. This, supposedly, is due to the fact that while these investors may have international as well as global prestige, they are still better known among industry actors in their geographical vicinity. Future research is important to determine the domain of generalizability of this finding.

In the cases of both Betelgeuse and Pollux, a US investor provided much support in internationalization to the United States, including a high degree of pressure. These investors had fit with the US market but the market was not the target internationalization market at the time of first entry, and according to our analysis, going into the US markets did not appear to be useful for the firms at the time. However, as we discuss in more detail below, the US market has subsequently become a target market for these companies. This points to the importance of the dynamics in the evolution of companies and of trying to reach a view to a firm's situation that is valid in the long term.

To summarize, the cases provide several examples of investors' significant support for internationalization and its planning. The most common business contributions relate to improved credibility, generating customer contacts and providing knowledge of the legal environment, opening doors to other parties such as business partners, and support in recruiting managers from the foreign location. Table 8.2 presents a summary and illustrations from our data of the contributions of CBVCs.

Table 8.2   Summary and illustrations of contributions of cross-border venture capitalists on the internationalization of the start-ups

Firm	Summary	Illustrations
Altair	Several of the investors took an active role in devising the internationalization plan of the firm in Summer 2001, when the firm underwent a major reorganization, but they did not actively exert pressure	'Naturally it helps a lot to have local contacts . . . especially in recruiting [they are valuable] . . . naturally the expertise of VCs could be better utilized if we decided to internationalize to a place where they have expertise'
Antares	The investors have helped in internationalization. However, because the management team is uncommonly experienced for a Finnish start-up, little advice has been needed. The American investor has given substantial help in the USA in the form of market knowledge and social capital.	'[The US investors] have provided information from the financial markets – and of customers and the state [of markets]. [They have given] information on competitors and the financial situation. [They have also given] information on potential partners and customers'
Betelgeuse	Support to internationalization has been focused in creating business cases and contacts. The support has been of help	'We [an investor] have introduced Betelgeuse to partner candidates, and we have sought out people [contacts]. We have brought in [name; a board member], who has built a European-wide retail chain'
Capella	The cross-border investor has provided significant endorsement benefits	'The most important benefit [that the existence of the cross-border investor has given] by far is their name . . . We are taken seriously, people are writing about us, and they are interested in meeting us'
Pollux	Investors provided their expertise in internationalization, helping for instance to obtain customers	'With [the fund], we got contacts to [the CVC investor firm managing the fund]' 'They may have helped us with [a customer] and [another customer], but they were not critical'
Procyon	The cross-border investor actively participates in the planning of establishing offices abroad. This investor has also provided contacts, and with those contacts, Procyon has discussed matters relating to internationalization	'The contacts [that the cross-border investor has provided] are useful. We have met many of them [other firms]' 'It was positive to get [the cross-border investor] involved. They provide contacts with Scandinavian

Table 8.2   (continued)

Firm	Summary	Illustrations
	and a common technology area. However, the foreign investor cannot provide significantly added endorsement, contacts to a large market, or proprietary-like business knowledge therein	[businesses relevant to Procyon] and some other contacts as well. And, they give us new insights'
Rigel	The Finnish investor had contacts with international venture capitalists, some of which then participated as investors. Investors have knowledge on financial matters that has benefited the firm, and they have provided a fair amount of endorsement	'[The local investor] had a lot of contacts with second round investors'

4.2   Negative Effects of Isomorphism

In addition to benefits, our data indicate that there are costs stemming from the participation of a CBVC. These costs arise because communication and travel from distant locations require more time, and because some venture capitalists drive portfolio companies in wrong directions as detailed in this section. Costs induced by CBVCs can be expected to outweigh the above-reviewed benefits in cases where the venture is pushed to internationalize to 'incorrect' markets, that is, areas that are not optimal for its growth. The lesser cost stemming from cross-border transacting may also outweigh the associated benefit from the existence of a cross-border investor – endorsement.

Regarding the target area of internationalization, the data hold that investors are likely to exert pressure to internationalize to the geographical location in which the venture capitalists manage the investment or have presence. If this location does not host a market that is optimal as a target market of internationalization for the venture, a pull to that market is naturally likely to cause disadvantages to the development of the venture.

Negative effects are dominant in Altair and Procyon. In addition, Betelgeuse and Pollux have both negative and positive effects and a high degree of conformational pressure. In Pollux, a cross-border investor first exerted pressure regarding the choice of the target internationalization market: Pollux founded an office in Munich 'because [the key investor] was from there'. Later on, a well-known venture capital investor from the

United States joined Pollux's financiers and was the lead investor on the round. The German investor lost interest and became passive. The new investor then wanted Pollux to move its headquarters to the United States. A respondent from Pollux stated: '[the new lead investor] required that the CEO would be stationed in the USA – the [US] office was established [at that time] due to their demands'. Multinational management was then hired and an American was recruited as the CEO. According to the founding entrepreneurs' view, this move to the United States was too quick, and the data support the notion that the firm's maturity for this significant an expansion was not fully developed.

Pollux has received investor pressure and negative effects of entering the US market too early, but the US market simultaneously has been a reasonable objective market at some stage, and the US investor has significantly helped Pollux there. To summarize, investors twice considerably affected Pollux's location choices, and some of that influence was damaging. However, the cross-border investor also extensively supported the US expansion by decreasing the firm's liabilities of foreignness. The investor provided, for example, social capital for obtaining customers. The case also provides a good example of the significant power that investors can exert.

In Betelgeuse, a US investor wanted the firm to establish offices in several locations, and special emphasis was placed on internationalizing to the United States, even though the country had not yet been identified as a target market for internationalization. However, while the investor exerted premature pressure to internationalize there, it also provided legitimization in the US market by enabling market access and providing contacts. The cases of Pollux and Betelgeuse exemplify how their key cross-border investor did not have good enough fit initially with the portfolio firms' target internationalization market, but the benefits from decreased liabilities of foreignness were perceived as useful in time, when the firms felt that their US presence was beneficial. Thus, they discovered that the market, where their cross-border investors had driven them, had become a target market, as stated above. A cross-border investor or other factors can influence a firm's situation so that new markets will be identified as targets in internationalization strategy.

In Altair and Procyon, negative effects dominate. In Altair, investors did not exert much pressure, but many of them were difficult to some degree. Because some of them – certain corporate venture capitalists – were mutual competitors, board work became troublesome. Additionally, Altair illustrates the increased transaction costs that cross-border investors bring with them due to requirements of communicating to distant locations and potentially culturally distant people. The investors did not have a notably good fit with target internationalization markets. In Procyon, investors have not exerted any strong pressure for guiding the internationalization in certain directions. This is not surprising, however, due to the fact that Procyon has only Finnish and Swedish investors. Similarly to Altair, the major effect of cross-border investors appears to lie in the increased costs of communication, meeting and decision making. The cross-border investor cannot significantly help internationalization via endorsement or providing foreign organizing knowledge in markets that are key target internationalization markets of the company.

Table 8.3 presents a summary and illustrations of the potential disadvantages that cross-border investors may bring with them. Note that in the table, we do not detail the negative effect of transaction costs. This effect is homogeneous across cases, and as intuition would suggest, present in all of them.

To summarize, the key finding of the section is that when there are CBVCs that actively participate in the management of the portfolio firms and do not operate from a geographic area central to the target internationalization market of the portfolio company, the portfolio company will encounter significant costs from cross-border investors that outweigh the benefits. These costs arise from CBVCs driving the firms to internationalize to 'incorrect' markets, that is, markets that are not included in the optimal set of target internationalization markets. At the least, cross-border investors generate relatively high costs from transacting. These costs are markedly present in each case study.

5. DRIVERS OF INVESTORS' POSITIVE OR NEGATIVE EFFECT ON INTERNATIONALIZATION

As a result of the empirical analysis, we developed a model of the role of CBVCs in the internationalization of their portfolio companies. The model is presented in Figure 8.1 and elaborated below.

First, the model holds that all cross-border investors introduce relatively high transaction costs because it is more expensive to communicate, make decisions, and travel between distant locations and people. Without target-market fit and active participation, this is the only effect that cross-border investors bring. However, when investors have a good fit with the target market of internationalization of the venture, they bring about not just transaction costs but also endorsement benefits from just being present with their name or by providing minor support. According to the simplified presentation inherent and sought in models, the benefit outweighs the problems that stem from high transaction costs.

Table 8.3   Summary and illustrations of potential disadvantages arising from the participation of a cross-border venture capitalist

Firm	Summary	Illustrations
Altair	Most cross-border investors have been active in absorbing inform-ation but not in contributing to the management as they were expected, creating transaction costs. Among the interest groups of the firm, some companies are competit-ing with each other and this often creates problems on the board	'They have different sort of interests' 'The relationship between [an investor] and [another interest group firm] cannot be very natural'
Antares	No visible problems except trans-action costs	
Betelgeuse	The cross-border investor has announced that it will give up venture capital investing. There is some uncertainty about what will be done with the investments. There was also pressure to expand to the USA prior to the USA becoming identified in the firm as a key expansion target market	'That [an investor] will quit [investing], will surely have an effect on some companies'
Capella	Since a key person at an investor firm left his employment, this firm has remained rather passive and seemingly uninterested	'We don't know what they want. We and [another investor] think that they might want to withdraw'
Pollux	The location for an office was chosen due to the office location of a cross-border investor. The investor later chose to support a competitor's technology and aban-doned Pollux. Another cross-border investor took a very powerful role in steering the company, and demanded that the HQ was quickly moved near its own offices. Some felt that after this the contribution of this investor declined sharply. Generally, the entrepreneurs were rather dissatisfied with the investors	'The Munich office was founded because [an investor] was from there' '[The investor] chose to no longer use Pollux's [technology] platform in their portfolio' '[The other investor] took a strong role . . . The office [near to this investor's offices, to which the HQ was moved] was established [already at that time] due to their demands. Pollux would have needed a more mature organization – [the investor] was in a terrible hurry' 'After the beginning, their guidance has remained at a rather low level'
Procyon	No visible problems except transaction costs	

Table 8.3   (continued)

Firm	Summary	Illustrations
Rigel	The contribution of the key cross-border investors has clearly remained lower than what was expected	'The benefit to us is not as great as one could have hoped for'

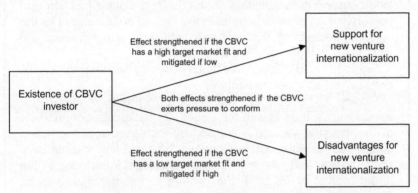

Figure 8.1   Effects of cross-border venture capitalists on new venture internationalization

When the key investor's fit with the target market is not good and they exert isomorphic pressure, they will drive the portfolio firm to internationalize to 'incorrect' markets. However, when the investor both exerts such institutionalizing pressure and has good fit, it can well provide international social capital and business and legal knowledge in the market, effectively decreasing the venture's liabilities of foreignness and legitimizing it in the new market. Additionally, our observations point to other ways in which venture capitalists can support portfolio firm internationalization, such as providing help in recruiting, scanning potential customers, and opening doors to technology partners and potential new financiers.

The model, as all models, is a simplified presentation. One assumption that is embedded in the discussion in this chapter is that the cross-border investor stays. Furthermore, we refer here to the target internationalization market as a market that currently has been identified by the venture as an objective. This consideration points to the relevance of time for internationalization decisions, as mentioned earlier. Even if the investor were in the correct market and actively participated in the management of the portfolio firm, the entrepreneurs may view steering towards starting internationalization as

---

BOX 8.1   FOUR FINDINGS CONCERNING THE ROLES OF CROSS-BORDER VENTURE CAPITALISTS IN THE INTERNATIONALIZATION OF THEIR PORTFOLIO COMPANIES

Finding 1   By their being present, CBVCs (a) increase the transaction costs carried by the venture, because it is more difficult and time-consuming to maintain contact with a distant location and person and (b) provide benefits in the form of endorsement for the venture, decreasing the venture's liabilities of foreignness and increasing its legitimacy in a new market.

Finding 2   CBVCs can use much power by exerting isomorphic pressure on an investee venture.

Finding 3   If CBVCs exert isomorphic pressure, they can – depending on their fit with the target internationalization markets of the investee venture – (a) convey increased legitimacy and decreased liabilities of foreignness by providing international social capital and relaying business and legal knowledge in the target market or (b) drive the venture to internationalize to an 'incorrect', non-target market.

Finding 4   (a) If a CBVC has good market fit, it can (i) provide general endorsement and, in some cases, (ii) convey increased legitimacy and decreased liabilities of foreignness by providing international social capital and relaying business and legal knowledge in the target market, depending on if it exerts isomorphic pressures to the investee. (b) If a CBVC does not have good market fit, then, depending on whether it exerts isomorphic pressures on the investee, (i) its presence may just show as increased costs or (ii) it can drive the venture to internationalize to an 'incorrect', non-target-market.

---

a premature step, as our case descriptions illustrate. The key findings of the study are summarized in Box 8.1.

6.   CONCLUSION AND IMPLICATIONS

In this chapter, we have examined the role of cross-border venture capital investors in the internationalization of investee firms that have their primary markets in foreign locations. The data came from seven ventures that have started in Finland and that have been financed by at least one cross-border investor, and were obtained primarily by conducting 49 interviews. The grounded theory methodology was used, resulting in four key findings and a model that illustrates them. Our main findings were that a cross-border investor's projection of conformational pressure and its fit with the venture's selected target internationalization market are important drivers of the investor's general effect on internationalization. At best, the investor may powerfully legitimize the investee, and at worst, can pull the investee into an 'incorrect' market.

Our findings concerning the effects of cross-border investors on portfolio ventures' internationalization have implications for the selection of cross-border investors. Both entrepreneurs and local investors should try hard to attract cross-border investors that can help the venture's internationalization as much as possible. To recognize which cross-border investors are likely to be the best ones, they should carefully examine the business of the venture and decide upon its internationalization strategy. Our findings strongly suggest that they should investigate objectives particularly in terms of the target markets of internationalization, and whether their new investor candidates are both willing and able to help them expand there. The findings indicate that cross-border investors are generally most able to help internationalization into markets from whose location they manage the investment. They may also be able to help internationalization to locations where they already have a presence. For instance, a US investor that manages a European investment from a European location can be of much help in expansion to the US markets.

In summary, it can be recommended that entrepreneurs and local investors accept cross-border venture capitalists that have significant presence in markets that are among the venture's key target markets for internationalization. These cross-border venture capitalists can significantly help the expansion effort by providing business and legal knowledge in the foreign market (foreign organizing knowledge) and contacts therein. In this way, they will help the venture to achieve a 'legitimate' position in a market in their vicinity – that is, to become accepted by businesses and people there. If the market that the investor knows, however, is not among those markets that are in the best interest of the venture (the investor does not have 'fit' in the markets of that best interest), significant disadvantages will naturally arise for the venture and the entrepreneurs.

Our findings also suggest that a cross-border investor can put significant pressure on ventures to become similar to ventures operating in the investor's vicinity. Whether the pressure will help or hinder the venture depends on the fit of the investor in the target internationalization markets.

If the cross-border investor does not exert much pressure, there still can be negative and positive effects for the portfolio firm. First, the costs of decision making, travelling and communicating are higher with cross-border interactions due to travelling time, time-zone effects and cultural differences. Second, the cross-border investor can, because of its name, provide endorsement to the venture especially in its vicinity but also internationally. Entrepreneurs and local investors should try to make sure that their cross-border investors have appropriate fit and are willing and able to transform the venture into a format compatible with the target markets. Cross-border investors should be able to provide significant endorsement, foreign organizing knowledge and foreign contacts. They should also accommodate and help reduce the negative effects of time zones, travelling time and cultural issues.

To conclude, an important practical insight that results from the results of this chapter is that prior to agreeing on cross-border investment rounds, entrepreneurial teams and local investors should carefully examine the internationalization objectives of the company, especially in terms of the target locations of internationalization and whether their new candidates for investors are both willing and able to help them there. In addition to financial capital, new investors should be able to provide endorsement, international contacts and foreign organizing knowledge. Investors, for their part, should search for portfolio companies whose business objectives can be, prior to agreeing on the investment, reconciled so as to be reasonable for both the investor and the investee.

NOTE

* For comments, we thank Richard Harrison, Leila Hurmerinta-Peltomäki, Henrikki Tikkanen, and the reviewers of the Academy of International Business Meeting 2004. A research paper of the authors that was based on the dataset employed in this chapter received the Haynes Prize of the Academy of International Business Foundation and the Eldridge Haynes Memorial Trust in 2004. Markus Mäkelä acknowledges financial support from the Emil Aaltonen Foundation.

REFERENCES

Baygan, G. and Freudenberg, M. (2000), 'The internationalisation of venture capital activity in OECD countries: implications for measurement and policy', OECD Working paper, Organization for Economic Cooperation and Development, Paris.
DiMaggio, P.J. and Powell, W.W. (1983), 'The iron cage revisited: institutional isomorphism and collective rationality in organizational fields', *American Sociological Review*, **48** (2), 147–60.

Oviatt, B.M. and McDougall, P.P. (1994), 'Toward a theory of international new ventures', *Journal of International Business Studies*, **25** (1), 45–64.

Sapienza, H.J., Manigart, S. and Vermier, W. (1996), 'Venture capitalist governance and value added in four countries', *Journal of Business Venturing*, **11** (6), 439–69.

Stuart, T.E., Hoang, H. and Hybels, R.C. (1999), 'Interorganizational endorsements and the performance of entrepreneurial ventures', *Administrative Science Quarterly*, **44**, 315–49.

9. Venture capitalists' communication and commitment: a practitioner's perspective

Dirk De Clercq and Vance H. Fried

1. INTRODUCTION

This chapter focuses on how venture capital firms (VCFs) can more effectively add value to their portfolio companies (PFCs) through (i) their *communication* both with the PFC and internally within the VCF and (ii) their *commitment* to the PFC. To the entrepreneur, VCF value added can be crucial to the success of his or her company (that is, the PFC). To the VCF, quality PFC investments are important to enjoy high returns. Although they are not the only driver of PFC performance, VCFs can often significantly enhance PFC performance by fulfilling a variety of 'value-adding' roles for the PFC. In fact, most VCFs spend more time providing these value-adding services to PFCs than they do evaluating new investment opportunities (Sahlman, 1990).

Prior research has identified several major value-adding roles for the VCF. For instance, venture capitalists play a strategic role as sounding boards for and generators of strategic initiatives, an operational role as providers of key external contacts for locating managerial recruits, professional service providers, or key customers, a personal role as friends, mentors and confidants, and a disciplinary role as directors who hold management responsible for meeting objectives and discharge management for non-performance (Sapienza et al., 1994; Fried and Hisrich, 1995). In this chapter, we examine the determinants of the successful execution of these roles.

Value added is the result of three things. First, the *quality* of the value-adding activities is crucial. For instance, is the VCF skilled in recruiting PFC management? Do leaders in the industry respect the VCF? Second, the *quantity* of value-adding activities plays an important role. For instance, how much time does the VCF spend on recruiting PFC management? How many industry contacts does the VCF provide? Finally, even if the VCF provides both quality and quantity, the management of the PFC must be

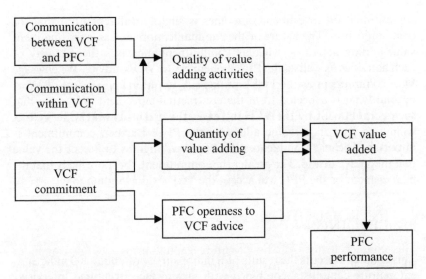

Figure 9.1 Venture capital firms (VCFs) creating value for their portfolio companies (PFCs)

open to accept the VCF's advice. Ultimately, VCF value added will increase PFC performance (Figure 9.1).

The main thrust of this chapter is that through their impact on the three factors mentioned above, (i) communication (between the VCF and the PFC, as well as within the VCF) and (ii) commitment (by the VCF to the PFC) ultimately play a major role in generating value added which then impacts PFC performance. Communication is important to VCF value added because it increases the quality of VCF value-adding activities. Communication creates learning opportunities for both the VCF and management of the PFC. The focus of this study is on the learning that takes place at the level of the venture capital *firm*, which then benefits the PFC by increasing the quality of the VCF's advice. We argue that learning from the investor's perspective not only involves individual learning efforts by venture capitalists but also is the outcome of interactions within the VCF. In other words, how much venture capitalists learn depends on not only their individual abilities to learn, but also the integration of skills and knowledge among colleague investors (Cohen and Levinthal, 1990). We explain how knowledge is assimilated and exploited within VCFs by examining the joint effect on investment outcomes of the communication *between* the VCF and the PFC as well as the communication *within* the VCF.

We also examine the role of commitment in generating VCF value added and PFC performance. The mechanism that underlies the effect of commitment on investment outcomes is slightly different from that for communication. The nature of the communication increases the quality of value-adding activities, whereas commitment increases the quantity of such activities as well as the PFCs' openness to VCFs' advice. We envisage VCF commitment as the VCF's propensity to put in a great deal of effort beyond what is expected from the contractual agreement. We argue that such commitment by the VCF increases the extent to which the VCF is willing to contribute value added to the PFC. Further, commitment is important because it influences the PFC's willingness to accept the value that the VCF can add. The greater the commitment, the more likely that the management of the PFC will accept the VCF's value-adding role.

2. FINDINGS

This chapter presents the results of a major survey of about 300 independent venture capitalists, combined with face-to-face structured interviews with several venture capitalists (see Appendix 9A for a summary of the study's methodology).

2.1 Role of Communication between VCF and PFC

Whereas it is generally known what the different activities are in which VCFs engage in order to support PFCs, the issue of how communication between the VCF and the PFC may help the VCF to exploit knowledge acquired from their interactions with PFCs is largely unexplored. Knowledge transfer between the VCF and the PFC may include informal contacts and formal meetings (De Clercq and Sapienza, 2001). Board meetings may offer an excellent opportunity for interaction including, for instance, the PFC's financial officer reporting to the VCF about the accomplishment of pre-set performance targets. Also, the variety of communication channels may reflect the quality of the exchange of information; that is, the use of different communication forms between the VCF and the PFC may enable the transfer of complex, rich and context-specific information, and facilitate problem solving. In other words, the employment of various interaction routines between the VCF and the PFC may enhance the VCF's capability of processing complex knowledge and understanding the knowledge received from the PFC.

We found that the insights gained by the VCF resulting from its interaction with the PFC increases the amount of value added by the VCF and, ultimately, PFC performance. A VCF may use the knowledge obtained from its interaction with a particular PFC to fill gaps in its own knowledge base and then apply this 'updated' knowledge to the benefit of the PFC. More specifically, the newly gained insights may help the VCF to more successfully execute the various roles it plays *vis-à-vis* the PFC (that is, its strategic, operational, interpersonal and disciplinary roles, see above) (Sapienza et al., 1994; Fried and Hisrich, 1995). For instance, close interactions between a VCF and a PFC active in the design of websites, may allow the VCF to detect similarities between this PFC and other PFCs in the Internet sector and therefore to update its understandings about this particular industry. These insights will then enhance the quality of the VCF's assistance to the PFC, for example, by referring the PFC to the most relevant external contacts, and ultimately enhance PFC performance.

In short, our findings suggest that the communication between the VCF and the PFC has a beneficial effect on VCF value added and PFC performance. The quality of such communication pertains to how much insight is gained by the VCF as the result of its interactions with a PFC. Our results indicate that interactions between the VCF and the PFC may provide the VCF with deeper insights into its existing knowledge base, and therefore enhance the extent to which the VCF can apply expertise to current (and future) PFCs.

Interestingly, the interviews we undertook with several venture capitalists indicated that fruitful interactions between the VCF and the PFC are not as such characterized by the venture capitalist systematically going over a check-list of issues that need to be taken care of, but rather by the promise to be continuously available and ready to communicate with the chief executive officer (CEO) about a myriad of aspects relevant to the PFC:

> For me, successful interactions include two aspects. First, I am asking the CEO continuously to go over his numbers, to check and update the sales plan, etc. Second, there is the mentoring process through which I try to improve the quality of the CEO just by being there, helping him with getting other investors, helping him to grow, finding new customers or suppliers, and insisting on the hiring of the right people. I think that if you would ask CEOs about their fruitful experiences with investors, they will tell you the same thing. The investor needs to be available and function as an adviser and sounding board, someone who helps you get through some important issues. I don't have a check sheet that says: if you make these decisions, success is guaranteed. But that is where the fun is, to help to figure out things. I always have fun!

At a more general level, our interviews gave some deeper understanding into several aspects for which the VCF's knowledge and insights can enhance the amount of value added and, ultimately, PFC performance. Some issues are rather industry specific, such as the amount of time it takes for a given product to be approved by the authorities for each of the subsequent test rounds, whereas other issues are more generic such as how to bring new technologies to the marketplace. For instance, one venture capitalist active in the health-care sector described the following aspects to be important in terms of what type of insights are needed by him in order to help his PFCs effectively:

> In our business, it is important to understand the regulatory process as well as the issue of reimbursement. That is, you need to be able to tell your company what steps need to be undertaken for reimbursement once the product has been approved. In addition, an important aspect, which is more generic, pertains to the channels of distribution. We all focus too much on product development, but at the end of the day, you have to figure out, in every market (i.e., not only in health care) how to get the product in front of the customer. Our insights can be very helpful here, e.g., in terms of whether corporate partnerships need to be involved, which distribution channels can be used, or whether you can market the products yourself.

Many also pointed to the importance of rightly assessing the quality of the key people in the PFC, not only before the investment decision has been made but also in the subsequent phases of the relationship. They felt that having insights into how to build and develop a management team and how to monitor the team's performance over time are invaluable drivers for value added:

> Even if you know what the venture market looks like, how the regulatory process works, or what the distribution channels are, you need to be knowledgeable about people issues as well. Along the way, you may have learned that different expertise is required to build different kinds of companies, and what it takes to drive a company through the different stages of development. In order to better help the company, you need to know all these things, that is, how to recruit people, how to build a team, how to motivate the founder. You really need to have this expertise. If not, you are screwed up.

2.2 Role of Communication within a VCF

The extent to which knowledge is assimilated *within* a VCF is also important. A VCF often has multiple general managers as well as a staff of associates who function as apprentices to the fund managers, and as such, these associates may also be involved in knowledge acquisition and interactions *vis-à-vis* the PFC (Sahlman, 1990). Communication among venture capitalists with regard to a *particular* PFC further strengthens the effect of the communication between the VCF and the PFC on investment outcomes.

Each of the partners within the VCF may have different backgrounds, and may have developed a variety of expertise in their capacity as private investor, entrepreneur or manager. That is, each of these individuals within the VCF may hold varying levels of knowledge relevant to the focal PFC (Sahlman, 1990). Therefore, effective communication among individual venture capitalists regarding that PFC will give the VCF broader access to and deeper insight into knowledge that is important to successfully assist the PFC. In order for the VCF to optimally exploit its knowledge base, it will have to combine and integrate knowledge from among various individuals within the firm.

At a more abstract level, communication within the VCF has an indirect rather than a direct effect on investment outcomes since such 'internal' communication will be useful to the PFC only when the VCF is able to detect the PFC's primary information needs through VCF–PFC interactions. Our results indeed suggest that internal communication among colleagues within the VCF regarding a particular PFC increases the impact of communications between the VCF and the PFC. More specifically, intensive communication within the VCF regarding a particular investment may help the VCF to internalize the new insights gained from the interaction with the PFC, and therefore ultimately increase the VCF's capacity to successfully utilize these insights to the benefit of the focal investment.

Interestingly, in the interviews many venture capitalists also suggested that not only the communication within a given VCF but also interactions among outside co-investors play an important role in increasing the effectiveness of VCF assistance. Indeed, venture capitalists often opt to invest together with other private equity investors in order to decrease investment risk and benefit from each other's expertise through syndication. The exploratory interviews indicated that fruitful interactions among the members of an investment syndicate are often perceived as very valuable for investment success. There may also be a learning process involved in terms of how to develop effective communications with co-investors during board meetings, as illustrated by the following quote from a venture capitalist:

> An important thing you need is a syndicate of co-investors. It is underappreciated how important it is to have the right people on the board, i.e., the right investors. If you have many people there with different objectives from you, you might end up with problems. Therefore, it is important to learn who you would like to have on the board with you, who you don't want, and how you manage the relationships among co-investors.

Further, although the question of how VCFs function internally was not the primary focus of this study, the exploratory interviews provided some interesting insights into this matter. One finding from the interviews was that most VCFs function in an informal rather than a formal way. Whereas some of the 'big' VCFs may be divided into different internal 'industry groups' who barely interact with one another, most VCFs have *all* partners and associates participate in their internal meetings. The following testimony provides an illustrative example of how internal communication takes place in many of the interviewed VCFs:

> Every Monday afternoon, the three of us go through every deal in our portfolio to see whether there is any need to better assist the companies. We also talk about the due diligence for new opportunities, to see where we are and what the next steps ought to be. We look at all the deals that have come in during the last week, and decide whether or not we want to pursue them. Of course we also have informal contacts with each other during the week, if we need to. That is the advantage of having a relatively small firm.

In addition, although some venture capitalists mentioned the existence of a somewhat formalized data collection procedure within their firm, most of these efforts pertained solely to information gathered during the due diligence process; that is, few efforts were undertaken aimed at systematically storing information regarding all prior and current deals. Interestingly, the opinions were divided in terms of whether a more formalized organization of data collection on PFCs would be beneficial or not, as illustrated by the quotes of two interviewees:

> I don't think we do a good job in storing data in a formal way. Once a month, we have a closer look at deals that haven't performed that well. Some people take notes, others don't. We don't have a formal database, but it would be a good thing to have.
> We pretty much know what is going on in our key PFCs based on our informal communication, which often just takes place in the hallway. I think there is question of how you get too formalized as a venture capital firm. When every decision has to be formalized, we may become too bureaucratic. We cannot be too institutional, or we would make a bad decision. This is not a business of consensus. In most cases, important decisions have already been made before the partner meetings. Also, only the lead partner for a given portfolio company decides about a potential CEO dismissal. The only issue where other partners come in is about whether to invest additional money in a given PFC.

2.3   Role of VCF Commitment

A deep commitment held by the VCF *vis-à-vis* its relationship with a particular PFC will lead the VCF to execute its value-adding roles more intensively and therefore increase the likelihood that the PFC will benefit from the VCF's assistance. For instance, the more frequent and intensive the contacts are between the VCF and its network partners with regard to the PFC, the higher the VCF's ability to leverage the knowledge embedded in its existing network towards the PFC. Another reason why commitment may pay off is that entrepreneurs' resistance *vis-à-vis* the VCF's advice will be lower. Such resistance is indeed often a reality given entrepreneurs' unwillingness to give up control over their company (Sahlman, 1990). To the extent that the VCF can generate relational power with the PFC, the PCF becomes more willing to accept the input of the VCF. A major issue in developing relational power is the amount of time the VCF is willing to commit (Fried and Hisrich, 1995).

In the interviews, several venture capitalists indicated that given their limited amount of time and responsibility over a myriad of PFCs, they could not give the same amount of attention to all PFCs; that is, they may become more committed to some PFCs compared to others. Our findings suggest that how much effort the VCF puts into the relationship with a particular PFC positively affects the ultimate success of the investment *beyond* the quality of interactions between the VCF and the PFC. More specifically, the VCF's commitment affects the intensity of value-adding activities as well as the openness by the PFC to the VCF's advice.

Interestingly, the relatively high value of the commitment scores across the sampled VCFs indicated that venture capitalists may often have a difficult time in trading off their efforts, or at least their emotional commitment, across their several PFCs. As one interviewee put it:

> One of the tricky aspects about our business is that once you have made a commitment, it is really a commitment. That means that you have to be prepared to do whatever it takes to help that company, if it is in your power. If the company gets in trouble, or it starts to grow very fast, we try to be responsive and to be involved as much as we can. There have been times when I spend as much as half my time on a single company, almost a daily activity.

2.4 Role of VCF Value Added

VCF value added has a positive impact on PFC performance. However, there are many other factors which impact PFC performance, either positively or negatively. A VCF can add a great deal of value to the PFC, yet the PFC may perform poorly because of problems within the PFC such as poor management, or negative events external to the PFC such as increased competition or a downturn in the economy. On the other hand, a PFC may perform very well even if the VCF adds no value. Thus, while communication and commitment have a positive impact on PFC performance, they certainly are not the only factors affecting PFC performance.

3.   CONCLUSION AND IMPLICATIONS

This study adds to our practical knowledge about how venture capitalists can improve the performance of an entrepreneurial company. We go beyond prior studies by highlighting the importance of *communication* between the VCF and the PFC as well as within the VCF, and the importance of the VCF's *commitment* to the PFC. We found that these factors indeed have a substantial influence on how effective VCFs' contributions towards their investee companies are, and ultimately affect the performance of these companies. We hope, then, that these insights will help practitioners, both entrepreneurs and venture capitalists, to create a better understanding of the creation and development of successful ventures.

Several practical implications follow from our findings. In the following paragraphs, we summarize how entrepreneurs as well as venture capitalists can learn from our results.

Our study suggests that for entrepreneurial firms seeking financing, the choice of a venture capital investor needs to go beyond financial considerations. More specifically, seekers of venture capital may benefit from being selective in choosing their potential investors. Some of the criteria that CEOs can use to increase the likelihood for a good fit with their venture capital provider are: whether there is some chemistry between both parties which allows for the development of good communication; whether there is an alignment between the two parties in terms of the entrepreneur's goals; whether the venture capitalists are willing to have open discussions with the venture's management team; and whether the investors are willing to commit themselves to their investment. Similarly, CEOs may also benefit from building and promoting a track record in terms of how *they* communicate with investors or other exchange partners in order to attract potentially strong investors.

Further, our findings indirectly suggest that, prior to investment, entrepreneurial companies looking for venture capital should have an insight into the benefits they seek in addition to the provision of capital, that is, they ought to have a clear understanding about which specific competencies they are looking for within potential investment firms. These insights may be particularly important if help is expected in functional areas that require specific knowledge.

The finding that investment outcomes depend, in part, on the amount of learning that takes place by the VCF as a result of its interactions with the PFC indicates that investors may find it necessary for their own survival to interact intensively with their portfolio companies, in that such quality interaction will allow them to renew, develop and transfer expertise in new and emerging domains. Furthermore, venture capital providers may increase their reputation among their peers and entrepreneurs by building an internal competency in terms of how to foster open and fruitful communication with PFCs.

Also, venture capitalists should be aware that in order to be competitive and valuable in quickly changing technological environments, they ought to promote within their firm a willingness to continuously update the existing expertise. Our interviews indicated that knowledge management within the VCF is often limited to data gathering during the due diligence process. An important challenge for VCFs may be to find an optimal balance between a systematic storage and utilization of the expertise developed by individual investors on the one hand, and the maintenance of a dynamic, flexible organization structure within the VCF on the other.

Finally, we found that the amount of effort the VCF devotes to a particular PFC increases the effectiveness of the VCF's assistance and ultimately enhances PFC performance. Entrepreneurs may often be unwilling to give up control over their company and be resistant in terms of the advice they receive from their venture capital providers. The findings of this study suggest, however, that when the venture capitalist shows his or her commitment to the entrepreneur, the latter may become more convinced about the potential value of the former's advice. Venture capitalists may therefore benefit from convincing CEOs that they are 'in the game' for the long run, and that they are willing to function as insiders of the entrepreneur's company rather than just as 'external' advisers. This may motivate the CEOs not only to provide more useful information to the VCF but also to exert maximum effort themselves in building effective relationships with their investor.

REFERENCES

Cohen, W.M. and Levinthal, D.A. (1990), 'Absorptive capacity: a new perspective on learning and innovation', *Administrative Science Quarterly*, **35**, 128–52.
De Clercq, D. and Sapienza, H.J. (2001), 'The creation of relational rents in venture capitalist–entrepreneur dyads', *Venture Capital: An International Journal of Entrepreneurial Finance*, **3** (2), 107–28.
Fried, V. and Hisrich, R. (1995), 'The venture capitalist: a relationship investor', *California Management Review*, **37** (2), 157–79.
Sahlman, W.A. (1990), 'The structure and governance of venture capital organizations', *Journal of Financial Economics*, **27**, 473–521.
Sapienza, H.J., Amason, A.C. and Manigart, S. (1994), 'The level and nature of venture capitalist involvement in their portfolio companies: a study of three European countries', *Managerial Finance,* **20** (1), 3–17.

APPENDIX 9A   METHODOLOGY

We empirically tested our arguments based on data collected through a survey filled out by US-based venture capitalists. The National Venture Capital Association enhanced the participation of the venture capitalists through the study's endorsement. In addition to the survey data, we also collected qualitative data based on face-to-face interviews with several venture capitalists. Despite the study's focus on the US market, we have no reason to believe that the principles upon which the theory for our findings are based should operate substantially differently compared to the European context. That is, our results are relevant to European as well as US-based entrepreneurs and venture capitalists who aim to increase the effectiveness of their relationships.

We used Venture Economics' database as the primary source for the selection of venture capital firms. Since we intended to include all VCFs that had been active since 1995 and since our database did not record systematically *all* investments that had been made by a given VCF, we included all US-based private VCFs that met at least one of the following criteria: (i) the database indicated that the VCF had undertaken at least one investment in the period from 1995 to 2001 or (ii) the VCF's website (when mentioned in the database) was still active. These criteria resulted in about 1400 VCFs being included in the study. The survey instrument was then sent to a randomly selected member of the top management team of the 1400 VCFs. The respondents were asked to choose one PFC that met the following criteria: (i) the initial investment in the focal PFC was preferably made in the period from 1998 to 2000, and (ii) the respondent was actively involved in the post-investment relationship with that PFC. To maximize randomness, we asked the respondents to select the one venture that met the above criteria *and* came first alphabetically.

We included several mailing rounds in the data collection process. As a result, our final sample (including about 300 VCF–PFC pairs) represents one of the largest surveys of venture capital firms. The research hypotheses were tested through hierarchical regression analyses. Since most of the data were collected through the survey instrument, we carefully checked whether common method bias was an issue; the results of Harman's one-factor test showed that this was not the case. Finally, we found that for all variables in the study, the goodness-of-fit indices (GFI, non-financial investment (NFI)) were higher than the minimum value of 0.80; in other words, the measurement items indeed represented 'valid measures' for their respective constructs.

One might argue that the assessment of ultimate investment success (that is, PFC performance) through a survey instrument filled out by venture capitalists represents, at times, a 'biased' view of performance, yet no single measure or index of start-up company performance has been found that can accurately and objectively compare PFCs across stages and industries. Furthermore, perceptions of PFC performance are crucial because ultimately VCFs' judgement of PFC performance determines whether VCFs will continue to support, refinance or abandon their investments. Further, the validity of the assessment of PFC performance by the lead investors is counted upon by other investors (for example, the syndicate members) and by VCFs' limited partners to determine the provision or withholding of huge investment amounts in follow-on investments in the PFC. Therefore, both venture capitalists and entrepreneurs should benefit from better understanding the factors that influence VCFs' assessment of PFC performance.

PART III

Private Equity and the Role of Public Policy in Europe

10. Private equity and the development of university spin-out companies

Mike Wright and Andy Lockett

1. INTRODUCTION

University inventions represent an exciting new way to create entrepreneurial ventures. The possibility of creating world-class businesses from the laboratory has captured the interest of governments and universities alike. Academics are increasingly seizing the opportunity to become entrepreneurs through spinning out ventures when just a few years ago this would probably have been anathema to many of them. Yet, ventures spun out from universities face major hurdles if these objectives are to be realized. A key constraint on growth is convincing venture capital firms and other equity financiers to provide funding. The problem is neatly summarized by a venture capitalist aiming to invest in university spin-outs:

> We manage \$2.4bn worth of investments. For us to make money we want to invest \$10m to \$15m first round, and that investment has to grow significantly to have an impact on our fund. Therefore, we are looking for the sorts of companies that can attract a lot of customers at a high price point, generate revenues and eventually IPO [initial public offering]. So far very few opportunities presented to us by universities for creating new spin-outs have met our criteria.

The problems associated with spin-outs obtaining risk capital is exemplified by the fact that only half of the spin-outs created in the UK in financial year 2002 were formed using external equity finance. Over two-thirds of universities did not create a new spin-out in this period but 30 per cent did create one or more with this source of funding. This highly skewed picture only partly reflects the distribution of the science base in universities. The largest single source of external finance for these newly created ventures was public sector funding provided by the government's University Challenge Fund (UCF) scheme which principally aimed to provide seed capital. Venture capital and business angel finance tended to be more in evidence when the venture had become more established. Those universities more active in spin-outs are more likely to see the

UCF and venture capital as important sources of finance than are other universities.

Our studies of recent developments in spin-outs provide important insights into the problems they face and possible means of resolving these difficulties. These studies have been conducted with university technology transfer offices, venture capitalists and entrepreneurs involved in spin-outs. (See Box 10.1 for details of studies.)

BOX 10.1   THE STUDIES

Qualitative data were collected using in-depth face-to-face and telephone interviews with representatives from 12 University spin-outs (USOs), as well as each of their financial investors and seven associated universities over the period from July 2001 to July 2002. These universities were selected on the basis that they are among the top 10 research elite universities in the UK and that they are actively pursuing a programme of university technology transfer. Each university was at a different point in transforming its policies, routines and incentive mechanisms towards commercialization through USOs. We selected a range of different ventures in terms of their technology and stage of development. Interviews were carried out with the head of the university technology transfer office (UTTO) – or equivalent – business development managers (BDMs) and the members of a spin-out company who had taken the venture through the process including both the academic entrepreneur and the 'surrogate' entrepreneur where applicable. We also gained access to the seed-stage investors in each of the USOs. In addition, we interviewed the head of each department from which the USO originated. The interviews lasted from one to two hours and were openly recorded and afterwards transcribed.

In March 2002, a survey on university technology transfer activities comprising quantitative and qualitative questionnaires was sent to the top universities in the UK as ranked by research income, accounting for 99.8 per cent. As the survey was conducted with the support of the two associations of technology transfer officers in the UK, the Universities' Companies Association (UNICO) and the Association of Universities Research and Industrial Liaison officers (AURIL), we were able to identify the most suitable respondent through their membership. We conducted an initial telephone exercise to identify the most suitable person to complete

the questionnaire. This person was typically the head of the technology transfer office or their designate. We received information
from 98 of these universities. We returned to these institutions in
the spring of 2003 and obtained full data on the level of their spin-
out activity in financial year 2002 from 124 universities. Tests
showed that the respondents were representative of the population of universities that are active in commercialization of university research.

For the study involving venture capitalists, the questionnaire was
sent in November 2003 to the 56 venture capital funds that identified themselves as being active investors in technology-based
small firms. We aimed to examine the attitudes and perceptions of
venture capital investors and to analyse the factors affecting the
supply of finance from venture capital funds for spin-outs. The
questionnaire sought both quantitative and qualitative information
as well as presenting the opportunity for respondents to offer
'write-in' comments. We received 27 fully completed questionnaires plus nine nil responses/partially completed returns.

In this chapter we examine the financing problems facing spin-out companies from the perspectives of the parties involved, that is technology
transfer officers, academic and surrogate entrepreneurs and venture capitalists. We aim to suggest means of addressing these problems. First, in
Section 2 we consider the problems in developing university spin-outs;
Section 2.1 adopts the perspective of the venture capital firm in screening
proposals; and Section 2.2 considers issues involved in getting spin-outs
ready to attract to venture capital investment. Section 3 examines the
nature of university technology transfer processes that will enable them to
create spin-outs that are attractive to external investors. Finally, we present
conclusions and recommendations for technology transfer offices, academic entrepreneurs, universities and venture capitalists.

2.   PROBLEMS IN THE DEVELOPMENT
OF SPIN-OUTS

Spin-out firms face a number of critical junctures in their development (Vohora et al., 2004). These critical junctures concern opportunity recognition, entrepreneurial commitment, credibility and sustainability. Over-
coming these critical junctures is an iterative process that involves addressing
deficiencies in networks, other resource weaknesses and inadequate internal

capabilities. At the opportunity recognition juncture it is necessary to conceptualize how a technological discovery can be best applied to satisfy a market need. To address this problem it is important for universities to devote more resources to increasing their social capital (networks) through developing and exploiting existing external partnerships, links and interactions with industry, venture capital firms and surrogate entrepreneurs so that academics and technology transfer offices may become better positioned to recognize entrepreneurial opportunities. At the entrepreneurial commitment juncture there is a need for a 'champion' committed to the entrepreneurial development of the spin-out who may be an academic or an entrepreneur from outside with commercial expertise, a so-called 'surrogate entrepreneur' (Franklin et al., 2001). The credibility juncture arises from university spin-outs' intangible initial resources, the typical lack of commercial track record of the founding entrepreneur, the effect of the academic culture and values, and the absence of clear policies on the commercialization of scientific discoveries, despite the rhetoric of senior university management. Universities can demonstrate the credibility of their spin-outs by presenting intellectual property (IP) as a potential portfolio of products, demonstrating proof of concept of technological assets, clarifying the route to market and profitability, being able to locate the venture off the university campus, and implement mechanisms to attract surrogate entrepreneurs. Traversing the sustainability juncture depended on a spin-out's networks for identifying opportunities and accessing resources, as well as integrating them with existing resources to create organizational capabilities that enables the spin-out to cope with the challenges of growth.

In enabling spin-outs to develop across these phases, UTTOs identify a number of important barriers that need to be overcome. Shortages of finance to undertake various crucial tasks are among the most important factors impeding the creation and development of successful USOs (Table 10.1). Access to venture capital firms and availability of proof of concept funding are especially problematical. A shortage of this area of funding in technology transfer offices may mean that potential spin-outs are unable to develop to the point where they meet investors' criteria.

2.1 Venture Capitalist Screening of Proposals

Spin-out ventures compete for venture capital with other private sector projects. Only a subset of venture capital firms invest in high-tech ventures and among this group not all will be active in the financing of spin-outs (Lockett et al., 2002). There are a number of significant differences between venture capitalists who are willing to invest in spin-outs and those who are not in terms of the criteria they use to reject an investment proposal. The factors are ranked in order of importance in Table 10.2.

Table 10.1   TTO views on factors impeding the creation of USO companies

Rank	Impediments	Mean value
1	Access to finance from venture capital firms	2.4
2	Availability of proof of concept funding for developing prototypes of the technology	2.5
3	The number of staff to manage the IP identification, assessment and exploitation process	2.5
4	Availability of proof of concept funding for conducting market research/analysis	2.6
5	Availability of proof of concept funding for conducting intellectual property right (IPR) due diligence	2.6
6	Incentives and rewards to attract commercial management to spin-outs	2.8
7	Availability of proof of concept funding for business plan development	2.8
8	Availability of resources to maintain patent applications	2.9

Note: Institutions were asked to indicate the factors impeding or promoting the creation and development of spin-out companies during FY 2002 on a scale from 1 to 5 where 1 = Strongly impeded; 2 = Impeded; 3 = No effect; 4 = Promoted; and 5 = Strongly promoted.

First, non-spin-out investors put greater emphasis on the size of the potential market when considering investment proposals. The difficulty many universities have in commercializing disruptive technologies emerging from blue-sky research is the lack of evidence on markets in which to apply the technology. An argument for spin-outs is that the technology is too early to license and so needs more development before value can be demonstrated to the market.

Joint ownership of an IPR with a university is significantly more important to non-spin-out investors. Investors feel uncomfortable about investing in USOs when the IPRs are licensed as opposed to being assigned in return for an equity share in the company. Therefore, some investors feel that there may need to be a 'clean break' from the university if the spin-out is to develop without interference in the running of the business. Furthermore, in the event of a spin-out failing to survive, the IPR within the venture may be the only valuable asset that can be recovered and sold off to another company. Universities tend to have a preference against assigning IP to spin-outs as they wish to retain some control over IPRs as well as expecting an equity stake in the spin-out in lieu of licence royalty payments. In this way, non-spin-out investors may perceive universities as retaining the potential to influence development of the spin-out without showing willingness to share risk.

*Table 10.2   Venture capitalist views on factors leading to rejection of
investment proposals: main significant differences between
spin-out investors and non-spin-out investors*

Factors of significant differences between spin-out and non-spin-out investors	Combined score	Non-spin-out investors	Spin-out investors
Size of potential market for applications of the technology	4.2	4.6	3.9
Stage of development of the product/service	4.1	4.7	3.6
Availability of a prototype/test data to demonstrate proof of concept	3.5	4.6	2.8
Difficulty in identifying key decision makers	3.4	4.1	3.0
Lack of formalized university technology transfer procedures	3.3	3.9	2.8
Requirement for service development to support customers who will use the product/service	3.0	3.7	2.4
Concerns over co-investing with public sector funds	2.9	3.7	2.4
Concerns over co-investing with universities	2.8	3.4	2.3
Joint ownership of the IPR with universities	2.6	4.0	1.9

Note: Respondents scored each factor as: 1 = Unimportant; 2 = Not very important; 3 = Quite important; 4 = Important; and 5 = Very important. A Mann–Whitney test was performed to analyse the differences between spin-out and non-spin-out investors.

It is very important for non-spin-out investors to see a prototype, such as an operational device, early versions of software, in order to assess the viability of the technology concerned. In contrast, spin-out investors place less importance on this issue and may invest at an earlier stage and work with the spin-out to achieve proof of concept. This also highlights the point that for non-spin-out investors to become more interested in funding spin-outs, proof of concept funding is essential. Without adequate resources to achieve proof of concept in particular it is unlikely that proposals for spin-outs will meet the investment criteria of non-spin-out investors.

Difficulties in identifying key decision makers in universities and a lack of formalized university technology transfer procedures appear to cause non-spin-out investors to reject investment. Universities may have the ability to make changes here that might help gain access to external funding, such as reducing the length of time taken to reach decisions.

Non-spin-out investors are less likely to invest in companies that lack plans to develop a sophisticated product and service offering that would

Table 10.3 *Venture capitalists' attitudes and perception of risks associated with investment in USOs*

Rank	Compared to high-tech companies, USOs are more likely to:	Mean value
1	• require the building of a management team	4.4
2	• require a longer investment time horizon	4.3
3	• require close monitoring	4.2
4	• require several rounds of funding	4.2
5	• have higher variability of return	3.6
6	• fail	3.6
7	• involve protracted pre-deal negotiations	3.5
8	• be small niche market companies	3.3
9	• pose valuation difficulties	3.2
10	• have financial structuring problems	3.1

Note: Respondents ranked each factor as: 1 = Strongly disagree; 2 = Disagree; 3 = Neither agree or disagree; 4 = Agree; and 5 = Strongly agree.

enable them to gain a significant share of business. Non-spin-out investors also place significantly more importance on their decision to reject an investment proposal, on the prospect of co-investing with public sector funds and universities. It may be that non-spin-out investors in particular are dissuaded from investing in spin-outs because of additional complications in negotiating terms and agreements with existing investors. The level of patent protection is an important consideration for investors since know-how and IPRs often underpin the competitive position of the product or service.

Not only do some venture capital firms not want to invest in spin-outs but all venture capital firms perceive that differences exist between spin-outs and other new technology-based firms. An important issue concerns perceived differences in risk between spin-out ventures and other high-tech ventures (Table 10.3). Venture capital investors have a different perception of risk and reward when considering investments in spin-outs and other high-tech companies. The most important requirement for potential investors involved having to build management teams. The length of time taken to realize substantial returns and the prospect of early investors having to go through a number of funding rounds before an exit can be achieved also make spin-outs less attractive investments. Although this condition may be ameliorated to some extent through improved efficiency in spin-outs, universities or technology transfer offices it is also simply a reflection of the early stage of development of most university technologies and the lengthy product development cycles in sectors such as life sciences. University spin-outs are perceived as bearing greater risk. Investing in spin-outs requires company development capabilities, experienced management and closer monitoring of an investment over a longer time horizon.

The importance attached to the quality of management teams reflects the need for assurance that the management team is capable of transforming a technological innovation into a sustainable business. An illustration of the importance of this problem is emphasized in the case of Virtual Reality (a pseudonym), a company producing virtual reality software for the manufacturing sector. The company failed repeatedly to raise equity finance. A venture capitalist who had reviewed their business plan and presentation commented:

> The technology was undoubtedly novel and world class [but] we questioned the academic team's commercial and managerial skills [and] expressed doubt about the senior academic's ability to attract new commercial people in order to grow the company.

Each time the academic entrepreneur in Virtual Reality met with investors to discuss his business plan he failed to demonstrate sufficient credibility, and was unable to secure any investment. In this particular case the academic had repeatedly failed to accept the feedback from potential investors and the technology transfer officer. As a result he could not attract a management of sufficient calibre with whom he was willing to work alongside, and was unable to show that any customers existed to buy applications of his technology. The venture capitalist summed up his frustration:

> The greater effort required to manage the risks involved in this type of deal is a real turn-off. When these guys come in here and I look them in the eye I want them to make me believe they can offer me a financial return. Why on earth should I invest in a business proposal that lacks a sound management team and shows no evidence of a market? We're not handing out research funding to academics here!

Frequently, the difficulty encountered by entrepreneurs in developing fundable investment propositions is that apart from intangible technological assets in the form of know-how and IP they had difficulty in showing that a team was in place that could demonstrate it was committed and able to create and deliver value.

2.2 Investor Readiness

Ventures need to be in position to be ready to meet the criteria for investors at different stages. For smaller funds the choice of whether to invest in a spin-out often depends on how quickly it can be taken to a stage at which co-investors can be brought on board to share the risks and supply funding in subsequent financing rounds. According to the venture capitalist that invested in 3G Wireless (a pseudonym), a venture aimed at designing low power consumption microprocessors and licensing the IP to manufacturers worldwide in the mobile telephone market:

> Academic entrepreneurs trying to raise seed venture capital for their spin-outs need to realize that seed stage investors are looking to fund deals that will enable co-investors to come on board within a year to eighteen months. . . . we are relying on the spin-out team to have created sufficient uplift in the valuation of the venture.

Lack of experience of technology transfer officers and their inability to add significant value to the venture can be detrimental to the ability of the spin-out to secure sufficient investment to achieve 'critical mass' before further rounds of financing are required. The amount of work involved in getting a proposition 'investor ready' for a larger venture capital firm is far greater than for a smaller investor, or a syndicate of business angels. For 3G Wireless it was difficult to attract sufficient interest from potential co-investors because not enough value had been added to the venture to progress it to a state of 'investor readiness' for the next stage of development. As the academic entrepreneur commented:

> With the seed money we'd initially raised we'd completed work on a prototype, carried out due diligence and protected the IP. However, we ran into difficulties when we needed to raise a further $2 million in venture capital to take the product to market. We knew precious little about how the product would perform for customers or even who our customers were! We weren't yet generating revenues to be able to entice new investors.

The result was that the entrepreneurs were forced to scale back their initial product and market strategies to concentrate on niche sectors that offered lower revenues.

3.   THE ROLE OF UNIVERSITY TECHNOLOGY TRANSFER PROCESSES

Resolving the problem of access to finance identified by technology transfer offices and the difficulties in investing in spin-outs reported by venture capitalists highlights the need to consider the role of university technology transfer processes. The availability of stocks of resource inputs and capabilities may be particularly important to the success of this process (Clarysse et al., 2005).

Stocks of resource inputs include the stock of technology to be exploited, external expenditure on IP protection and the number of people employed in the technology transfer process. Capabilities involve the routines possessed and developed by universities in relation to the generation of spin-outs that are more likely to create wealth.

These capabilities can be identified in terms of business development capabilities and routines for incentives and rewards to commercialize the technology, including the royalty regime.

Our analysis of UK universities shows that the following *stocks* of resource inputs are important drivers of universities' creation of both spin-outs and of spin-outs that attract equity finance (Table 10.4). In particular, external expenditure on IP protection was found to be consistently significant in the creation of university spin-outs. The number of staff in the technology transfer office *per se* and the stock of experience in terms of the number of years a university had been engaged in technology transfer were not a significant influence on spin-out creation once the capabilities of staff are taken into account.

In terms of the capabilities and routines of the university we find that the business development capabilities are significant. Indeed, the influence of business development capabilities is significantly greater for those spin-outs with external equity investments than for the creation of spin-outs *per se*.

Table 10.4   Influences on spin-out creation

Influence	USOs	Equity-backed USOs
Total research expenditure	No significant effect	No significant effect
Expenditure on IP protection	Significantly increases	Very significantly increases
Total TTO staff	No significant effect	No significant effect
No. years involved in TT	No significant effect	Significantly increases
Business development capabilities of TT staff	Significantly increases	Very significantly increases
Royalty regime	Significantly increases	Significantly increases
Incentives & reward system	No significant effect	No significant effect
Has established links with external financiers	No significant effect	No significant effect
Presence of a medical school	No significant effect	No significant effect
Presence of a science park	No significant effect	No significant effect
R&D intensity of business in local region	No significant effect	No significant effect

Source: Authors' analysis.

These findings emphasize that it is not so much the number of technology transfer staff that is important but their expertise.

The components of the business capability development process suggest that the creation of capabilities related to clear processes for conducing IPR due diligence and the creation of spin-out companies, and the availability of adequately trained staff are important determinants of a university's success in creating spin-outs and externally equity-backed spin-outs. The nature of the royalty regime had a significant influence on spin-out creation but the nature of incentives and rewards regimes were not significant: the greater the academic inventor's share of royalties, the more likely was there to be spin-out creation.

4. CONCLUSION AND IMPLICATIONS

Our extensive studies of venture capital firms involved in the funding of spin-outs, university technology transfer offices and spin-out companies themselves have enabled us to identify both the problems in attracting venture capital for spin-outs and potential means of addressing these problems.

Investment proposals that are more likely to be considered positively by venture capital investors are likely to satisfy the following: a clear route to market for applications of the technology; size of potential market for applications of the technology; stage of development of the technology and availability of a prototype/test data to demonstrate proof of concept; number of rounds of follow-on investment required; level of patent protection of intellectual property; and strong management team. Universities and academic entrepreneurs that can meet these investment criteria will be more likely to secure funding for spin-outs. Based on our analysis, we offer the following recommendations for the parties involved.

Technology transfer offices and academic entrepreneurs need to develop sufficiently attractive investment opportunities if spin-outs are to secure anything other than a small amount of financial investment from venture capitalists who are able to offer substantial involvement. Where academic entrepreneurs and technology transfer offices do not have sufficient expertise to create the investment propositions that sufficiently meet the criteria of professional investors, the spin-outs that are created by universities lack a specific commercial focus, and are likely to be little more than 'technology development vehicles'. This raises issues concerning the building of appropriate teams to develop the spin-out proposition.

The significance of IPR protection expenditure in the context of spin-outs with external investment signals the need for technology transfer offices to make sure intellectual property is clean, well defined and protected before trying to raise external equity finance. This finding also emphasizes the lack of internal skills in this area, as has also been noted in reviews of technology transfer practices. This suggests that technology transfer offices need to develop sufficient expertise in the area of IP protection as well as adequate budgets to finance the cost of external advice in this area.

A related issue concerns the need for technology transfer offices and investors to resolve questions of the ownership of the IP. On the one hand, because of the amount of risk involved in commercializing inventions, venture capital firms may seek assignment rather than licensing of IP to a spin-out as a condition for investment. On the other hand, technology transfer offices may reluctant to do this as it may reduce further economic benefit from continued scientific developments. To some extent this is an issue of UTTOs and academics being realistic about the value of their IP at very early stages and the classic need for founders to 'let go' if they are to reap significant gains. It also may reflect risk aversion on the part of venture capitalists. A way forward would seem to be to negotiate unrestricted rights for spin-outs to use the IP to develop commercial products in a particular field but for universities to be able to claim back ownership if the venture fails to become established.

The importance of business development capabilities that we have identified means that universities need to think of the commercial experience and skills of their staff if they are to create spin-outs that create wealth. Hence, university policies to pursue growth in the size of UTTOs without also focusing on the capabilities base may not be conducive to meeting revenue objectives for technology transfer activities. Our findings stress that approaches to professionalize UTTOs by government and professional associations, need to emphasize the broad array of business skills.

Universities are making changes to fill skills gaps by recruiting individuals with business experience from industry and through the provision of training courses by industry associations. A central issue concerns whether the training of existing technology transfer officers will yield the desired results or whether there is a need to recruit such officers with an appropriate private sector background, including experience of starting a business. The frequent complaint by venture capitalists about the lack of investor readiness of spin-outs compared to other early-stage high-tech ventures suggests an important difference in the background of the entrepreneurs and their advisers and lends support to the notion of recruiting more technology transfer officer skills from the private sector. This raises implications for how universities should attract and retain technology transfer officers. If universities are constrained to remunerate these officers in line with other elements of university bureaucracies, they may be unable to attract staff with the more entrepreneurial capabilities required to stimulate and develop successful spin-outs.

At the university level there is a need to improve decision-making processes regarding venture capital investment in spin-outs. Universities may need to develop standard procedures and processes for creating spin-out companies in order to speed up decision making and offer greater transparency in the decision-making process. Universities also need to address the difficulties faced by venture capital firms in identifying key decision makers and having to deal with multiple stakeholders. This may be a function of the clarity of development of a university's objectives and strategies towards spin-outs. Some universities may adopt a very conservative approach because of their concerns about accountability for public funds. It is clear, however, that those universities that are more active in spinning out companies adopt an approach to decision making that is more in line with commercial business practice (Lockett et al., 2003).

Universities might also do more to establish and nurture good links with private sector companies to gain a better understanding of how to develop scientific research into commercial applications. These links may also help universities in deciding whether an invention is most appropriately developed as a licence or a joint venture with a private sector corporation rather than as an independent spin-out with venture capital backing.

Our findings also indicate that venture capital firms need to put greater emphasis on ensuring that universities understand their requirements. Rather than focusing on a transactions approach, there may be benefits for venture capital firms to develop relationships with universities that are likely to generate a flow of possible investment opportunities. Some venture capital firms are already adopting this strategy, but a longer-term perspective may need to be taken that is involved in developing potential deals from an early seed stage.

Just as there is a need to develop the skills of technology transfer officers, there is also a need for venture capital investors to acquire the specific skills and understanding required when assessing spin-out proposals; these skills still seem to be in short supply.

REFERENCES

Clarysse, B., Wright, M., Lockett, A., van de Elde, E. and Vohora, A. (2005), 'Spinning out new ventures: a typology of incubation strategies from European research institutions', *Journal of Business Venturing*, **20**, 183–216.

Franklin, S., Wright, M. and Lockett, A. (2001), 'Academic and surrogate entrepreneurs in university spin-out companies', *Journal of Technology Transfer*, **26** (1–2), 127–41.

Lockett, A., Murray, G. and Wright, M. (2002), 'Do venture capitalists still have a bias against technology based investments?', *Research Policy*, **31**, 1009–30.

Lockett, A., Wright, M. and Franklin, S. (2003), 'Technology transfer and universities' spin-out strategies', *Small Business Economics*, **20**, 185–200.

Vohora, A., Wright, M. and Lockett, A. (2004), 'Critical junctures in the growth in university high-tech spin-out companies', *Research Policy*, **33**, 147–75.

11.   Dynamics of university spin-out companies: entrepreneurial ventures or technology lifestyle businesses?

Richard T. Harrison and Claire M. Leitch

1.   INTRODUCTION

According to a recent commentary in the (London) *Financial Times* (11 May 2004, p. 13) by Jonathon Guthrie,

> [There are] growing doubts surrounding university spin-outs, the 1,000 or so new businesses set up to commercialise university research. . . . the government has been using taxpayers' cash to stimulate the spin-outs that it uses as proof it is succeeding in making boffins more commercially-minded. But . . . there were no figures . . . to prove that costs – including public investment – were less than the sales of products, intellectual property or spin-out equity. The businesses could as easily have been destroying value as creating it.

Furthermore,

> [There is a] need for better measurement of the returns produced by university spin-outs. Without this, it is impossible to see whether they are creating value – leaving the debate on whether spin-outs beat collaboration or licensing to fall back on the voodoo of anecdotal evidence.

A central theme in economic, industrial and technology policy discussions across Europe in recent years has been the link between wealth creation and competitiveness in a knowledge-driven global economy and the exploitation of scientific and technological developments in scientific laboratories and universities. Indeed, the higher education sector is increasingly seen as having a significant role to play in regional economic development. Not only are universities important engines of technological development and growth, but they can potentially act as catalysts for the enhancement of employment opportunities (either directly or indirectly) for local industry, most particularly in the high-technology and knowledge-based sectors.

One means by which it is believed that university-based knowledge can be utilized is through the establishment of university spin-out companies, especially as universities increasingly seek to contribute to their region's economic development. This is because spin-outs tend to locate near their parent organization and thus, their economic benefits in terms of job creation and taxable wealth tend to accrue locally. This is in contrast to technology transfer from a university to a large cooperation where benefits are more likely to be transferred out of the immediate region. As well as being viewed, by some commentators, as an efficient means by which to transfer technology from universities to industry, the creation and growth of spin-out companies can not only provide employment for a university's graduates but in some cases can also contribute to university revenue. This is particularly the case in the UK where increasingly within the HEI (higher education institute) sector, which has faced a reduction in central government support, there has been a shift in the UK from a grant to an exchange economy in higher education. Attention has thus been focused on commercialization activities, including the development of spin-out companies, as a means of generating alternative sources of income.

Largely immediate financial pressures and the need to generate income in the short term, therefore, have driven the realization of the potential of a university's intellectual assets, and so attention had tended to focus on activities such as contract research and licensing and not on spinning out companies. This is because employing the spin-out route as the prime means of generating income tends to be seen as requiring more effort over a longer term and for more uncertain returns. For this reason the argument for the wholesale adoption of this strategy by HEIs does not appear to be very compelling, as some recent commentators (see quotations above) make clear. Indeed, generating an income stream for the university from this activity is not always of prime consideration for university management. Instead, reasons advanced to explain involvement in spin-out company formation, and also licensing technology, included retaining close links with business, an opportunity to 'market test' ideas when appropriate and access to the best and most current equipment. In addition, for the more research-intensive universities in the UK engaging in this activity is viewed as a means of attracting and retaining the best staff as well as supporting the university's core research mission.

The risks and problems inherent in establishing spin-out companies should not be underestimated and they represent only one route in commercializing a university's intellectual property. In appropriate circumstance such ventures can make a significant contribution to economic prosperity – for instance, in the last six years, Imperial College, London has been involved in spinning out 53 companies, one of which, Turbo Genset, was recently valued at £740 million, and there is a trickle of spin-outs now raising venture capital or listing on public markets. These remain a small minority of all spin-out companies, however.

The key challenge is to ensure that where it is considered that spinning out a company is the most viable option to adopt, it is structured and managed so that its potential is fully realized. Many factors influence the extent to which a spin-out company survives in the first instance, and whether it grows into a venture that can make a significant economic contribution. While there is a substantive literature on which types of firms or individuals succeed in spin-out company formation, it is important to consider which features lead to success in spin-out company generation, especially as the indicators of success in this area are not well defined. Specifically, the number of spin-outs alone is an insufficient indicator of success because this ignores their initial scale as well as their potential to grow and survive. Given that many spin-outs do not grow, it is vital to understand those factors likely to hinder spin-out growth and those that can contribute to their success.

In this chapter we report on research which analyses the processes governing the origins, establishment and growth of university spin-out ventures. Specifically, we explore the growth dynamics of university spin-out companies using data gathered from in-depth semi-structured interviews with the founders and/or chief executive officers (CEOs) of a population of spin-out companies in one university within the UK. The chapter is structured as follows. First, we consider the recent trends in spin-out activity within the UK. Second, we review the debate on the specific difficulties and challenges associated with spin-out company formation. Third, we summarize the case study methodology adopted in this chapter and profile the research site. Fourth, based on an analysis of the data gathered we explore the extent to which 'technology lifestyle' businesses exist within the spin-out population of this particular university and identify the key dimensions on which high- and low-growth entrepreneurial technology lifestyle business differ. Finally, we identify the implications of this phenomenon of technology lifestyle businesses for universities, technology entrepreneurs and policy makers with an interest in regional and national economic development.

In sum, increasingly, universities are being seen as important engines of technological development and growth which can act as catalysts for the enhancement of employment opportunities and the development of high-technology and knowledge-based sectors. One means by which it is believed that university-based knowledge can be utilized is through the establishment of university spin-out companies, especially as universities increasingly seek to contribute to their region's economic development. This is because spin-outs tend to locate near their parent organization and thus, their economic benefits in terms of job creation and taxable wealth tend to accrue locally. In this chapter we conclude that many university spin-outs are more like technology lifestyle ventures than entrepreneurial businesses, and are limited in growth potential by the aspirations of the founders, the composition of the initial management teams and the resource endowments of the ventures. Accordingly, the majority of these ventures will make only a minimal contribution to the development of the regional economies in which they are located.

2.　RECENT TRENDS IN SPIN-OUT COMPANY FORMATION IN THE UK

Recent surveys of commercialization activity in UK universities suggest that university technology transfer is an activity at which the UK is very good. Indeed, per unit of funding, UK universities are completing more technology licence agreements than their US counterparts as well as spinning out nearly twice as many new companies. Despite this activity there has been an overall decrease in spin-out company formation, possibly as a result of difficult market conditions for technology-based companies and redressing the balance between spinning out companies and licensing technology to existing companies as an optimum route to commercialization.

However, spin-out numbers alone are not a useful indicator of the impact of commercialization activity. While some university spin-outs have been successful, the net return to universities from the majority is comparatively insignificant. Indeed, it is difficult to ascertain how successful spin-out companies are as hard data on how research translates into commercial success is not available in the UK, and there is a need for information on factors such as the longevity, scale and equity value of each venture as well as the relationship among spin-offs, start-ups and licensing income.

While the recent introduction of university commercialization surveys has gone some way to addressing this problem, insufficient data means that it is still not possible to make international comparisons with respect to spin-out company success. Instead, they suggest that it might be more meaningful to draw comparisons about the quality of spin-outs. One mechanism by which this might be achieved is by examining the number of new ventures that are created using external equity finance as well as the amount of external equity that a new spin-out company might receive. Other variables (for instance, sales, turnover and increased employment) are also appropriate guides to the success (and by implication the quality) of a firm.

Indeed, if these factors are taken into consideration then the picture with respect to spin-out company development in the UK can be considered in a comparatively positive light: total turnover and staffing of all active companies have continued to rise, suggesting that company growth is occurring. This may be a reflection of a change in emphasis from increasing the number of new companies to a focus on enhancing their viability. Nevertheless, the UK figures still suggest that the majority of spin-outs remain small, with those surviving for more than three years still averaging only about 10–15 employees.

3. SPIN-OUT COMPANY FORMATION: CHALLENGES AND DIFFICULTIES

In addition to the significant barriers that any new venture potentially has to overcome, spin-out companies encounter additional entrepreneurial challenges beyond those faced by new high-tech ventures in general. Specifically, many spin-out companies are formed, not by classic entrepreneurs, but by an entrepreneurial academic, differentiated from the academic entrepreneur in that the former may not necessarily be growth oriented or aware of his/her business's innovation and development needs. Furthermore, as the academic might still be working within the university, growth of the spin-out company might not be his/her first priority. Indeed, the academic may not have either a unique idea or a high need for achievement in this area but may instead be pursuing more independence or looking for ways in which to overcome dissatisfaction with his/her current role. Further, university spin-outs generally tend to be founded primarily on the basis of some technological advance rather than on the presumption of some sort of competitive advantage based on marketing, sales or distribution. Indeed the founders of such ventures tend to have limited business experience. Collectively, these point to two fundamental difficulties with spin-outs: first, the specific challenges and obstacles encountered in the evolution of an initial idea in a non-commercial environment to becoming established as a competitive rent-generating firm; and second, the conflicting objectives of key stakeholders which may adversely impact upon a new venture's ability to move from one phase to another.

4. METHODOLOGICAL APPROACH

The case study reported in this chapter represents part of an ongoing research project which focuses on the spin-out company activity of one of the longest established technology transfer organizations in the UK, Queen's University, Belfast, Northern Ireland. The research focuses on the development and growth of approximately 50 per cent of the spin-out companies established with the support of the university's technology transfer company, QUBIS Ltd. In-depth, semi-structured interviews were conducted with the chief executive of the commercial holding company of Queen's as well as with the founders and/or CEOs of the university's spin-out companies. These interviews lasted on average two and a half hours and were conducted over an eight-month period from September 2003 to April 2004. Following a resource-based perspective the interviews focused on identifying the importance of a number of key resources on the development of these ventures. Specifically, information was gathered on company demographics (formation date, employment and sales history, technology and market orientation), the founding process (the research and technology foundation, the relationship with the university, the career path of the founding team) and the business development process (formation and development of the management team, recruitment of key personnel, product development and diversification, development of market and customers, access to finance, social capital networks).

5. RESULTS

The spin-outs included in the sample are highly diverse (Table 11.1): they cover a range of sectors (five each in software and biotech/medical, with others in electronics, manufacturing and environmental consultancy), and have been established for varying periods of time – eight are recent foundations (2000 or later), while three were established in the late 1980s. This pattern reflects the recent rise in the level of spin-out company formation in the UK. Given the age profile, it is not surprising that the majority of these spin-outs are small in employment terms: only four companies employed more than 40 in 2004. However, the relationship between company formation date and size is not absolute: software company K has grown rapidly, despite its recent formation (reflecting the fact that this is a second-order spin-out of an existing spin-out rather than an organically growing new venture, and company J has remained small, reflecting in part its continuing emphasis on local and national consultancy activity. What these figures do suggest is that there is, first, little evidence to suggest that university spin-out companies (even the relatively successful ones) will provide a substantive contribution to economic well-being, and second, that where benefits are being realized, even on a small scale, these are achieved only over the long term. (For example, company D, established and trading for around 25 years, has just been listed as one of the fastest-growing inner-city-based businesses in the UK: this very recent growth – 35 per cent compound since 1997 – after a long period of stability, has been capped by flotation on the Alternative Investment Market in late 2004 with a placing valuation of £23 million.)

With one exception (company B) these spin-outs are based on the exploitation of very small portfolios of protectable intellectual property (in terms of patents and other forms of IP protection), and in the exceptional case this large IP portfolio is not yet associated with above-average venture performance. In the software sector, particularly with a services rather than products orientation which is characteristic of these companies, the absence of formal IP protection is understandable, but it is less evident why this relatively low reliance on strong IP portfolios should be characteristic of the other companies in the sample, and it calls into question the extent to which these companies, for the most part, compete on the basis of specific complementary intellectual assets. This suggests that more detailed examination of the asset specificity of university spin-outs should pay more attention to generic issues of intellectual assets and their exploitation than to formal IP and its protection *per se*.

With the exception of company K, those spin-outs that have grown since start-up have done so by developing a strong market presence in markets outside the UK, and company K, as a recent second-order spin-out based on the development of a new software product, is aggressively targeting the non-UK market.

In terms of the perception of university support for spin-out companies, it is clear that there has been considerable variation, depending on the precise area of potential support required by the spin-out venture (Table 11.2). For most companies, the university-provided services which are most highly regarded (rated as 'important' or 'very important') are in the areas of general encouragement to exploit technology, in clarifying the legal IP position (not a surprise, given the university's own interests in this matter), providing IP protection through support for patent filing activities, providing pre-company-formation business advice, and in their general support. Much less valued was the university support for identifying the market opportunity for the technology, technology development, explanation of alternative exploitation options and career options for academic entrepreneurs. What clearly comes across, therefore, is a university role characterized by general exhortation and specific IP-related advice, which is less extensively backed up by detailed advice and services in the strategic and operational development of the technology into a commercial venture: this confirms suggestions elsewhere that there is an ongoing gap in the provision of support in the commercialization process between proof of (and

Table 11.1   *Characteristics of case study spin-out companies*

	Company					
	A	B	C	D	E	F
Year of formation	1996	1990	2002	1989	1993	2002
Employees in 2004	10	45	1.5	111	5	4
Sector	Software	Electronics	Manufacturing	Electronics	Biotech	Medical
Initial patents filed		14	1		1	1
Current patents held		30		4		1
Initial licences		100s				
Current licences						
Other IP protection					trademark	
Initial market/ customer		Broad base	Global	University research labs	Global	Hospital
Current primary customer		Broad base	Research institute	Labs and OEMs	Labs and research institutes	
Projected size		$2bn	£60k	US$60m		
Number of customers	Not trading	150	3		Many	Not yet trading
Market share		1% of US market		US$3m sales	Full	
% market in UK		10%		<10%	8%	
% market ex-UK		90%		>90%	92%	

				Company				
G	H	I	J	K	L	M	N	O
2002	2002	1986	1987	2001	2003	2001	1999	2002
7	15	170	11	75	4	0	5	1
Software	Bio-tech	Software	Environmental	Software	High-tech textiles	Bio-tech	Software	Medical
	1				Not yet	4		
	3							
				trademark				
Higher education	academic labs	Medium /large organisations	Government agencies	Large computer companies	Europe haulage sector	Effluent/ waste treatment	Higher education	Medical education
Higher education	SMEs biotech	Medium/ large organisations	Environment & health sectors	Large computer companies	Europe haulage sector		Higher education	Medical manuf.
Quite large	Over £1m	Limitless		Limitless	£200m		Quite large	Large
9	Over 60	>100	350	>100	Not yet trading	Little trading activity	5	
1%	Full?	Unknown	18–20%	<1%			1%	
90%	Little	Unknown	100%	99%			50%	40%
10%	Most	Unknown	0%	1% but target to increase			50%	60%

Table 11.2   University support for spin-out companies

Service provision from university	Role					
	Not played	Very unimportant				Very important
		1	2	3	4	5
Identified 'market opportunity' for technology	7	5	0	0	1	2
Assisted in technology development	6	3	2	2	0	2
Explained exploitation options (licensing, spin-out)	6	2	0	0	3	4
Laid out career options (i.e. academic vs. entrepreneur)	6	2	2	2	3	0
Provided pre-company-formation business advice	2	1	1	1	4	6
Provided IP protection (filing activities for IPR)	4	1	0	0	4	6
Clarified legal position of IP (who owns what)	4	1	1	0	2	7
Encouraged/supported founder to exploit technology	2	1	1	0	1	10
Provided strategy for spinning out company	3	1	0	5	1	5
Promoted spin-out to external commercial agents	2	2	2	1	5	3
Overall support by university in company formation	1	2	0	1	5	6

protection of) concept and commercial venture development which is not currently covered by the university technology transfer office. Unless there are other actors in the network providing this support and advice (and in peripheral regional economies where university technology transfer offices play an economic development role rather than or as well as a technology transfer role, this may be problematic) there are resulting constraints on the development of these ventures.

Most respondents identified benefits from being associated with the university/technology transfer office. For many, these benefits were in the form of the advice and support offered through the start-up process, described by company C as 'looking after the company's interests while a VC may not'. Others pointed to the provision of business services (for example, office support), and networking and communication opportunities that made a contribution to the development of the business through identification of partners, staff and market opportunities. For a small number of respondents there was also a benefit in terms of credibility and reputation: the association with the university to some extent overcame or helped to overcome the liabilities of newness that constrain new ventures.

On the other hand, there are also disadvantages of being associated with the university, identified by almost half of the respondents. For some, these were represented in the tensions between spin-out company development and other aspects of the academic role (teaching, departmental administration and research) and in interdepartmental tensions within the institution. For others, the association was deemed responsible for problems in resource acquisition strategies, in terms of attracting outside investors and the investment capital required (company C; M) and good business-experienced recruits (company B). What is not clear from these few cases where resource constraints have been identified is the extent to which they will influence negatively the development of the company. Company B has grown to above-average spin-out size over 14 years,[1] and the other two companies are still very new: the problems in accessing external equity, and the potentially negative signals that association with the university sends out, are, however, consistent with the wider UK issue that spin-outs have problems in accessing external equity.

6.   CONCLUSION AND IMPLICATIONS

This initial analysis of the nature of the spin-out company development process has suggested that there are considerable differences among spin-outs in terms of their development. For the most part, spin-outs from UK universities appear to start and remain small, even where they are serving international rather than local and national markets. Even where they do grow, over a period of a decade or more, they still remain relatively small in employment terms. This raises a number of issues. From a public policy perspective, this suggests that spin-out companies are at best only going to make a minor contribution to economic development: they do not, on present evidence, represent a platform for sustained economic transformation. From the university sector point of view, spin-outs are not likely to be a major source of income, as compared to licensing or other technology transfer activities. From a research point of view, this initial evidence suggests that the identification of the determinants of the overall performance of university spin-outs over the long run, and of variations in that performance, is an important area for further more detailed research. In so doing, and in the light of the evidence on the services provided by the university to spin-outs, that research could usefully focus on the resource acquisition strategies of spin-out companies: access to adequate resources in terms of finance, skilled personnel, advice and business development support and entrepreneurial capital are crucial to venture development.

NOTE

1. Since this chapter was drafted, company B has been acquired by a $1 billion US company for around £11 million, with the prospect of some job losses to follow the change of ownership.

REFERENCES

Leitch, C.M. and Harrison, R.T. (2005), 'Maximising the potential of university spin-outs: the development of second-order commercialisation activities', *R&D Management*, **35**, 257–72.

Shane, S. (2004), *Academic Entrepreneurship: University Spin-offs and Wealth Creation*, Cheltenham, UK and Northampton, MA, USA: Edward Elgar.

Tang, K., Vohora, A. and Freeman, R. (eds) (2004), *Taking Research to Market: How to Build Successful University Spin-outs*, London: Euromoney Books.

Vohora, A., Wright, M. and Lockett, A. (2004), 'Critical junctures in the development in university high-tech spin-out companies', *Research Policy*, **33**, 147–75.

For Information and Analysis of University Spin-out Activity in the UK

Hague, D. and Oakley, K. (2000), *Spin-offs and Start-ups in UK Universities*, London: Universities UK.

Higher Education Funding Council for England (2004), *Higher Education–Business Interaction Survey 2001–02*, Bristol, UK: HEFCE.

Lambert, R. (2003), *Lambert Review of Business–University Collaboration*, London: HM Treasury.

UNICO/NUBS (2004), *Annual UNICO–NUBS Survey on University Commercialization Activities. Financial Year 2003*, Nottingham, UK: Nottingham University Business School (NUBS).

12. Through a glass darkly: new perspectives on the equity gap

Gordon Murray and Dimo Dimov

1. SEED CAPITAL: WHERE ARE WE AT?

It has been represented to us that great difficulty is experienced by the smaller and medium sized businesses in raising the capital which they may from time to time require, even when the security is perfectly sound.

1.1 *Plus Ça Change*

But many small businesses with high growth potential still find it difficult to access the risk capital, and particularly the equity they need to fulfil their ambitions. These lost opportunities represent both an economic cost through reduced productivity growth and job creation, and a social cost to the communities within which they trade.

The two above statements could be successive paragraphs in a contemporary report on the state of financing of small and medium-sized enterprises (SMEs) in 2004. But there is one difference – 72 years! The first quotation comes from the former British Prime Minister, Harold Macmillan, reporting the results of a government committee charged to look at the parlous state of finances for smaller businesses in the United Kingdom post the Great Depression of the 1930s. This 1931 report is still remembered for its coining of the ever-green term – 'the equity gap' – to describe the wholesale unattractiveness of small firms to investors regardless of the underlying quality of the enterprise. The second statement is from a would-be UK prime minister, Gordon Brown, writing an introduction as the Chancellor of the Exchequer to a 2003 HM Treasury report on the equity gap.

1.2 Three Score Years and Ten

For most of the succeeding period of a biblical life span between Macmillan and Brown, small firms have remained in the policy shadow of large business. It was only as a result of catalytic research work carried out in the 1970s by David Birch of the Massachusetts Institute of Technology that the true importance of SMEs to a vibrant economy started to be appreciated. Birch showed using US data that small businesses were the major engine of an advanced economy's employment growth. Not only did existing and new SMEs buffer the downsizing effects of large firms but they also were the largest contributors to net employment growth. Birch's work predated the small business-driven technology revolution, which would become synonymous with the locations of Palo Alto, Southern California and Route 128 Boston. But by the late 1980s virtually every developed economy in the world had started to realize that small businesses were not the 'also ran', vestigial rump of a mature economy but the bedrock on which a large and important part of a nation's future economic and innovative foundations were firmly grounded. Accordingly, the 1990s saw a deluge of reports, initiatives and programmes which exhorted as diverse groups as schoolchildren, large corporations, government departments and university professors all to become more entrepreneurial. By the New Millennium, entrepreneurs such as Steve Jobs and Richard Branson had become the new Moses indicating, if much of the hyperbole was to be believed, a promised land based on unrestrained free market access and burgeoning new enterprises.

New business is risky and a majority of start-ups deservedly die within one to three years of their birth. But an entrepreneurial society requires investors to take risks in order that the stream of spectacular new ideas that will fuel the future reinvigoration of an established economy can obtain the critical first pounds (or euros, dollars or yen) on which the nascent enterprise relies. Thus, the renaissance of the importance of SMEs, particularly as a major means of ensuring technological innovation, has been intimately associated with the growth of *venture capital* finance, often termed 'risk capital'. The continuing and dominant success of the US economy in the commercialization of new technologies has become the biggest single argument for the value of new venture finance. America's ability to create large numbers of both individual (business angels) and institutional (venture capitalists) conduits to invest in high-potential but also highly speculative ventures has been one defining characteristic isolating the USA from otherwise comparable European economies.

1.3   A European Paradox

Europe has not kept up with the USA as a powerhouse of new technology commercialization. For Europe, the problem is simply put. If an investor is to be rational, regardless of whether acting as an individual or an institutional investor, he or she would invest in management buy-outs

(MBOs) and other later-stage private equity instruments. The rational investor would eschew any invitations to invest in early-stage and particularly new technology investments. Over the period since the 1980s that the British Venture Capital Association (the UK is the largest venture capital/private equity industry outside of the US) has been able to collect performance figures, early-stage investments have seen a 'cash to cash' internal rate of return (IRR) of 4.7 per cent p.a.. Over the same period, large MBOs have registered a return to investors of 16.4 per cent p.a. In the last 10 years, the normal cycle of a closed-end fund, the returns to early stage in the UK have been *minus* 10.6 per cent compared to larger MBOs *plus* 17.7 per cent. In the US, the results are reversed with early stage/seed investments providing a far more attractive return at 39.8 per cent p.a. than all MBOs at 8.5 per cent p.a. This disparity in comparable investment performances, particularly in the domain of early-stage technology enterprises, has had inevitable consequences. As one senior UK venture capitalist replied when asked if his fund invested in British high-tech start-ups: 'If it has got coloured wires and a plug, we won't touch it!'.

That European investors have followed this trenchant (albeit jaundiced) advice is incontestable. And the earlier the stage of investment, the greater the disparities between supply and demand. The UK industry association does not even attempt to record seed capital statistics that have become rounding errors in an aggregation of all stages of venture capital and private equity investment. As the UK government's own statistics show, the UK has the worst early-stage/later-stage ratio of risk capital funds available of any major economic region in the world.

The result of this relative dearth of early-stage equity finance is likely to be a major contributor to the widespread policy concern – termed the 'European paradox' – that European scientists may produce world class IP (intellectual property) but the fruits of their endeavours are then captured and capitalized by American and Asian businesses which more effectively and quickly commercialize innovative opportunities regardless of their origins. A modern economy lacks early-stage venture capital and the presence of experienced investors able to nurture and grow new technology enterprises at its peril.

1.4 Small Is Ugly

In contradiction to the popular catchphrase 'small is beautiful', the patent truth seems to be that small is downright ugly when it comes to fund management within venture finance. As UK and European funds have increased in size they have abandoned seed and then start-up finance. Large funds have migrated to large later-stage deals in Europe. The huge increase

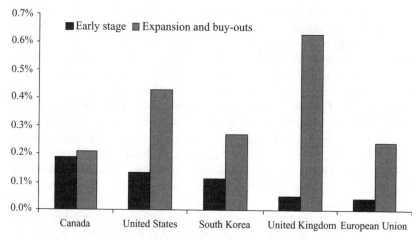

Source: OECD Venture Capital Database (2002).

*Figure 12.1   An equity gap? Venture capital by stage as a proportion of
          GDP, 1998–2001*

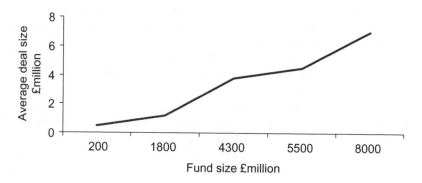

*Figure 12.2   Relationship between UK venture fund size and average deal
          size, 1984–2002*

in funds allocated to venture capital as an alternative asset class has exacerbated this trend. A managing partner faced with a fund of half a billion dollars in a closed-end fund, a five-year investment horizon and a requirement for net IRRs to the limited partners in the high teens/low twenties, faces some very clear market signals. He or she feels little need or obligation to dabble in a sprinkling of 100:1 outsiders needing set-up finance of less than a million dollars and a 10-year period of grace before any returns are confirmed. As a consequence, as the size of the fund under management by venture capital firms increases so will the minimum and average amounts invested in first-round portfolio companies.

This association between fund and deal sizes is in part because of the tyranny of indivisible fixed costs. A good investment executive in a competitive professional labour market does not cost any less because the finance is to be invested in small rather than large tranches. The 'due diligence' necessary to assess the prospects of a novel technology-based enterprise is no less costly if its founders are seeking $500,000 seed funding as opposed to $10 million expansion finance. Further, a general partner on a 2 per cent (of total fund value) fee income and a carry of 20 per cent of net capital gain has a very clear rationale to go for as large a fund as possible. When these structural disincentives to investing small sums of money are aligned and compounded with the greater uncertainties and risk of early-stage technology investing, there appears an unassailable logic for investors to abandon the types of speculative investment opportunities that have led in the past to venture capital-financed industry revolutions in the form of Microsoft, Apple, Cisco, Amgen, eBay and so on.

1.5 Government Policy Responses

The supply of seed capital is universally perceived as problematic. It is, and has remained, the venture capital industry's 'skeleton in the cupboard' in all regions outside the USA. Government has sought to address these equity gap issues by both supply- and demand-side initiatives. Ironically, the single most common contemporary policy response is to use the experience of the US government's Small Business Investment Companies programme (SBICs) to increase incentives to private investors. The logic of these 'equity enhancement' schemes is that with the state providing subordinated finance to commercially sponsored early-stage funds, the positive returns to private investors can be leveraged sufficiently to attract their commercial interest and involvement. Typically, government funds are invested first and repaid last thereby increasing further the leveraged returns to the preferential, private investors' equity contribution. In a smaller number of cases, the private investors are also offered guarantees covering part of their equity exposure to the fund.

2. TIME FOR A NEW PERSPECTIVE ON SEED CAPITAL?

In order to understand how seed capital *really* works, it is necessary to explore the character and dynamics of those funds and to understand the behaviour of investment executives who have actually undertaken this challenging investment activity. This empirical observation is particularly important as only a minority of venture capital general partners actually engage in any early-stage investment activity at all. To this end, the authors engaged on a set of interlinked and contiguous research activities. Specifically, the problems were address from three separate but related levels of analysis:

> *Tier 1: Venture capital funds* – using secondary data sources from an established industry database.
> *Tier 2: Top management teams in venture capital firms* – using empirical observation prior to collecting secondary data including archival materials.
> *Tier 3: Individual investment executives in venture capital firms* – using the results of findings from an experiment on business school participants.

2.1   Who Actually Makes Seed Capital Investments, and Does Fund Size Matter?

At the most aggregated level, we explore the actions of venture capital funds that have demonstrated a minimum threshold level of interest in seed investments. Our analysis reviewed the portfolio compositions of nearly 3000 funds worldwide between 1962 and 2002 – a period which represents virtually the totality of venture capital investment activity to date. We focus only on funds that have made at least 10 portfolio investments, thereby reducing the bias that may emerge from including less active funds. We have also excluded venture-backed, internet-based investment from our analysis in order to remove the 'bubble effect' of the dot.com era. There are two parts to our analysis: (i) identifying the factors that distinguish the funds that *have* made seed investment from those that have not; and (ii), for those funds that have made seed investments, identifying the factors that contribute to a higher intensity of such investment.

Our results highlight several important associations and interactions. In particular, the longer the VC fund has been in existence, the more prepared its managers are to make seed investments. Cumulative experience appears to matter in an activity known for its difficulty. The study discovered that some of the largest and most established VC funds, particularly, in the US, had also made the most seed investments (see Table 12.1). This fact is not well known with many industry observers believing that most seed funds are small specialist entities.

However, the relationship between scale and seed activity is not linear. An 'inverse U' shaped curve exists indicating that, as a fund increases its portfolio numbers, it also invests in more seed deals until an inversion point when increased portfolio size becomes associated with an overall decline in

Table 12.1   Sources of venture capitalists' risk in seed (technology) investment

Source of risk	Internal (I) or external (E)	Characteristics of risk
Management risk	I	The entrepreneur and management team possess insufficient skills to grow the company effectively and profitably
Market risk	E	The product/service introduced by the firm is insufficiently attractive to the marketplace to generate the necessary sales revenues, the target market is too small, or competitors react too vigorously
Technology risk	E	The proposed novel technology or its application proves unsuccessful by either not working or producing insufficient benefits to potential users
Pricing risk	I/E	The investor overestimates the terminal value of the enterprise and, thus, under-prices the contribution of equity provided
Financial risk	I/E	The enterprise does not generate the scale of revenues or profits to meet the investment return targets of the investors and/or cover debt interest

seed activity. Conversely, the relationship between total invested capital and seed activity is a 'U' shape. As funds get larger they make fewer seed deals but this relationship changes and the very largest funds are, once again, active seed investors. However, given the scale of these very large funds, their seed activity frequently remains largely hidden.

These non-linear relationships suggest that there exists both a minimum and maximum scale efficiency in making seed investments. In particular, a fund can be too small (as measured by the value of funds under management) for seed activity. Also as a portfolio gets larger in number of firms, the level of seed activity increases and then declines with further portfolio growth. These findings have significant policy implications for the state as a major funder of seed capital. Our results also highlight the importance of *exploration* by the fund manager. Investors in new technologies need to know what innovations may be imminent – heralding both continuous and discontinuous change – from a close observation of research activity. A new technology might have enormous effects on society and, as such, present huge commercial opportunities provided that the investor was closely attuned to and observant of the changing technology landscape. Thus, when viewed in this context, our results suggest that seed investing may be an important mechanism for investors to stay at the forefront of industry developments. In essence, for the larger funds with substantial technology interests, seed capital investment may be justified as much as an *advanced intelligence* activity as by any capital gain consequent on the relatively unimportant levels of monies invested.

2.2 Assessing Deal Flow: What *Really* Counts?

Talking about the 'behaviour' of a fund is to anthropomorphize an intangible object. The fund is a legal envelope that defines the rights and responsibilities of a number of investors or limited partners regarding the husbandry of a fixed sum of money for investment, and any returns flowing from that investment. Funds *per se* can neither invest nor disinvest. Executive decision making, including the crafting of fund strategies and subsequent investment allocations or exits, is the responsibility of the professional staff, that is, the general managing partners of the venture capital firm. In order to gain a deeper understanding as to why professional investors who adopt certain strategies may be more or less open to making seed investments, we move beyond the fund to also focus on the actions of the *top management team* level of venture capital firms.

The data for this second study embraced the investment history of 112 US venture capital firms over a six-year period (1996–2002) and included building a detailed account of the prior experience (education and industry experience) of the firms' top decision makers. We were interested in understanding in detail what type of investments individual venture capital firms had made, and the performance outcomes of these investments. In addition, we sought to distinguish between different areas of expertise among general partner investors and their consequent effects on the selection and success of their portfolio companies.

We judged the expertise of the management on both specialist and general competencies:

- *specific human capital* or *requisite expertise* pertained to knowledge and skills related to financial risk appraisal and management;
- *general human capital* pertained to knowledge and skills that are more detached from the context of portfolio management.

Finally, we examined the degree to which the status and reputation of the VC firm, facilitated or deterred its involvement in seed investing.

We found that the type of experience (that is, human capital) of the top management team members affected the focus of the portfolio both in terms of (i) the selected development stages and (ii) the relative success of the portfolio investments. More specifically, we found that an executive background in finance-related industries was *negatively* associated with the proportion of early-stage (that is, including seed) investments accepted by the funds, and positively associated with prevention of bankruptcies (rather than with the achievement of successful exits) among their portfolio firms.

These results led us to speculate that prior experience mattered in terms of how risky investments were perceived, chosen and managed. Thus, although investment analysis and selection is popularly conceived as a set of *learned* skills that are both objective and quantitatively verifiable, our results can be seen to challenge this simplified logic. They indicate that the venture capital firms' senior investment executives are rather less objectively rational and rather more subjectively *conditioned* than would at first be expected. The national venture capital industry associations go to great lengths to publicize the professional and objective nature of the decision processes, which determine how their members allocate scarce funds to excessive numbers of claimants. Industry statistics show that only around one in a hundred applicants for risk capital is likely to be successful. Over half of all entrepreneurs seeking initial funding from professional venture capitalists are likely to be refused after a cursory inspection of their proposal. Venture capitalists' processes are frequently held up as exemplars of professionalism for other groups of investors. In comparison, business angels are sometimes criticized for not being so objectively rigorous in their analyses and selection processes as formal venture capital firms. Our findings would suggest that venture capitalists' claims to a professional objectivity might be aspirational rather than necessarily factual.

In addition to highlighting the importance of the educational and professional backgrounds of the managing partners for explaining the intensity of seed investing, we also found that a venture capital firm's social network position further moderated its pattern of seed investing. We found both positive and negative influences at play. On one hand, for high-status firms, executives with a finance industry background were even less interested in early-stage businesses. Status appears to encourage conservatism. On the other hand, venture capital firms with strong reputations built upon previous successes were sensitized to take a more risk tolerant approach towards accepting early-stage firms. This suggests that two opposing forces may be in play: namely, a venture capital firm's high social position may restrain its willingness to invest in unproven industries or companies, while its past successes (and thus accumulated slack resources) may propel it towards experimentation. Essentially, higher fund status and positive investment performance experience makes firms become either more focused on or likely to minimize risk (the 'banker approach') or likely to maximize success (the 'entrepreneur approach'), respectively. The fund's behaviour to new opportunities is likely to change over time, depending on previous performance and the general partners' consequent willingness to take risks or play it safe.

This insight from the venture capital firms' management teams then served to inform our third study, which looks at the decision processes of the individual team members.

2.3   In the End It Is Individuals Who Say 'Yes' or 'No'

Just as funds are actually managed by investment teams, these teams are similarly composed of *individual* investment professionals. Whether or not an opportunity is recognized and acted upon initially requires the attention and then the direct engagement and commitment of an analyst. The analyst's recommendation will subsequently be sanctioned or rejected by an investment team or committee in a standardized investment process. Thus, the committee's decision necessarily requires the prologue of individual action. The inter-relationships between prior experience, risk perception and management action have to be measured against the actions and preferences of individual participants. They cannot be fully inferred from a group-level study. Accordingly, our third study involves experimental work at the individual investment executive level. It elaborates specifically on the key issue of the relationship between prior experience (of the investor) and the origination of seed deals.

In particular, we examine the initial *screening* of potential venture capital deals and relate the outcomes to the prior experience of the investor. Our focus on deal screening decisions was motivated by the fact that, as noted, over 90 per cent of incoming investment proposals to a venture capital firm are eliminated within a very short time. There is a 'two-tier' selection process and investors do not waste valuable time, experience and the cost of expert opinions on pursuing due diligence for all but a minority of deals that are perceived as potentially attractive. We suggest that there might be an observable relationship between the characteristics of the deals that do make it through the 'first cut' and some stable predispositions of the individual investor making the selection decision. We start from the assumption that the screening decision maker seeks to either maximize success (upside focus) or minimize risk (downside focus). In order to model individual action more credibly, we include both the investor's technical expertise and learning style as elements to the decision model. Underpinning our assumption is a testable hypothesis that previous experience influences current actions.

In order to capture the interplay on the selection process between the characteristics of potential deals and the influence of investors' prior knowledge and experience, we conducted a specially designed experiment. Ninety-three MBA students, members of the Private Equity Club in a major international business school, were invited to respond to three deal scenarios representing varying degrees of uncertainty. Our knowledge of the students undertaking the experiment allowed us to cross-reference their selection actions with the individuals' preferences and expert knowledge.

The results showed that positively responding to uncertain and risky deals depended on: (i) the level of deal uncertainty and (ii) a particular combination of domain-specific knowledge and learning style. In high-uncertainty deals, the effect of domain-specific knowledge on deal screening is negative regardless of the investor's learning style, with a steeper slope for investors with *accommodative* learning styles, that is, focused on success maximization. These findings also suggest that high-uncertainty situations may be quite overwhelming with risk concerns becoming paramount. This is consistent with a managerial perspective of risk, that is, stressing the need to avoid losses as well as a risk aversion in the domain of gains. Investors bereft of information or relevant personal experiences of a new enterprise are likely to react negatively. Further, investors with expertise are likely to be increasingly negative at both high and low levels of risk. The former is too scary and the latter is likely to be unattractive for reasons of insufficient profits. This finding is likely to induce a pained response among most entrepreneurs. It appears that they are 'damned if they do' (go for high risk/high reward) and damned if they don't (go for low risks/low reward).

The entrepreneurial applicant for venture funds certainly cannot predict the learning style or domain experience of the person who will appraise his/her application for funds. Very often, the applicant will never meet the person charged with filtering out the unmanageable stream of new business proposals that most venture capitalists experience on a daily basis. All the applicant can do is to try and pitch his/her ideas to funds which have a clear level of experience in the entrepreneur's chosen enterprise area. It may well be highly desirable to use a professional and knowledgeable intermediary to ensure access to appropriate investor firms. Further, funds that have in the past been successful investors are more likely to be sympathetic to high risk/high reward ideas if they remain in their field of competence. However, such knowledge is not widely available.

Table 12.2   Twenty-five most active venture capital firms investing in seed capital, 1962–2002

Name of VC firm	No. seed investments	No. portfolio companies	% seed in portfolio	Invested capital ($000)	Nationality VC firm	Year founded
Crosspoint Venture Partners	109	233	46.8	1,575,698	USA	1978
New Enterprise Associates	104	662	15.7	4,009,177	USA	1975
Kleiner Perkins Caufield & Byers	100	488	20.5	2,732,371	USA	1973
Mayfield Fund	74	433	17.1	2,220,803	USA	1970
J.P. Morgan Partners (FKA: Chase Capital Partners)	72	1352	5.3	8,685,709	USA	1967
Sequoia Capital	50	469	10.7	2,160,099	USA	1975
U.S. Venture Partners	49	322	15.2	1,747,813	USA	1980
Domain Associates, L.L.C.	46	175	26.3	902,362	USA	1981
Institutional Venture Partners	45	304	14.8	1,592,411	USA	1960
Ben Franklin Technology Partners, The	41	70	58.6	21,963	USA	1995
Draper Fisher Jurvetson (FKA: Draper Associates)	38	191	19.9	833,224	USA	1983
Oak Investment Partners	38	403	9.4	2,944,157	USA	1960
Mohr Davidow Ventures	36	168	21.4	818,542	USA	1983
St. Paul Venture Capital, Inc.	36	209	17.2	1,009,378	USA	1988

Table 12.2   (continued)

Name of VC firm	No. seed investments	No. portfolio companies	% seed in portfolio	Invested capital ($000)	Nationality VC firm	Year founded
Sevin Rosen Funds (AKA: Sevin Rosen Management Co.)	35	200	17.5	1,052,892	USA	1981
Asset Management Company Venture Capital	34	190	17.9	278,385	USA	1974
Accel Partners	33	307	10.7	2,040,098	USA	1983
Venrock Associates	33	331	10.0	1,318,561	USA	1968
Bay Partners	32	163	19.6	501,221	USA	1976
Bessemer Venture Partners	32	405	7.9	1,623,480	USA	1961
Sitra (AKA: Finnish National Fund for Research and Dev.)	32	90	35.6	17,169	Finland	1987
Sutter Hill Ventures	32	227	14.1	630,548	USA	1965
Alpha Capital Venture Partners, L.P.	31	50	62.0	73,667	USA	1982
Centennial Ventures	31	178	17.4	1,020,368	USA	1980
Greylock	29	340	8.5	1,172,839	USA	1968

Source: VentureXpert database published by Thomson Financial.

3.   CONCLUSION AND IMPLICATIONS

In summary, we can observe that increasing fund size is not necessarily a barrier to seed capital investment. Our results provide evidence of minimum scale efficiency. Thus, there are strong arguments that governments should redirect their activities to supporting not only new specialist early-stage funds but also to encouraging the incremental seed activity of large established venture capital firms. In Europe, such imprecations by government are not likely to be universally welcome by either larger funds or their limited partners. While the venture capital community almost universally accepts the need for seed funds, there is also a consensus that *someone else* should do it. When it comes to seed capital, most European investors are 'nimbys', that is, not in my backyard. European venture capitalists all too often continue to lack the ideological commitment or the skill sets of their more technologically literate US cousins.

In order to comprehend the nature of seed investment, and perhaps influence its supply, it is evident that the entrepreneurs seeking seed funds must be both proactive and savvy. They need to understand the behaviour and background (education and industry experience) of the venture capital firms' top management teams. The histories of the team members influence both their preferences and their investment behaviour. Investors' experience also influences the degree to which they can affect the successful outcomes of the enterprises into which they have committed equity finance. Given the two prevailing strategies of maximizing success or minimizing failures, the investors in VC funds face a dilemma. Investment executives from a finance industry background prefer to avoid risky, seed-stage investments. They have neither the industry skills nor the aptitude for such an investment activity. These investors are not likely to be the initial sponsors or backers of the next generation of global winners comparable to Microsoft, Cisco or Amgen. However, just as they are less likely to see very successful investment exits, they are also less likely to have their portfolio companies go bankrupt. Poorly informed on technology and cautious, these archetypal financiers fulfil every prejudice of the technology community!

Our results also show that two personal experience factors, that is, specific human capital and learning style, are crucial for effectively responding to potential deals containing a high degree of uncertainty. These insights may help in the design of effective seed capital investment activities. For the state to intervene effectively in supporting the initial financing of early-stage firms, it may need to allocate as much resource to deepening the human capital of the early-stage investment community as to providing a large part of the total funds, which are hazarded on new enterprises. Seed capital is a peculiarly challenging investment activity. And governments who see knowledge as a critical strategic asset of a modern economy will similarly have little choice but to continue to find means for its encouragement. We can offer no easy solutions. Seed capital is, and will remain in the foreseeable future, a hard and stony road to travel for both investors and governments alike.

13. Innovation, technology transfer and the equity gap: a European perspective

Tom Schamp*

1. INTRODUCTION

The Lisbon European Council of 2000 established the strategic goal for the European Union to become the most competitive and dynamic knowledge-based economy in the world by 2010. In fact, Europe's researchers are among the world's leaders in many areas of technological research and development but much of their exploitable work never reaches the market-place, or it does too slowly. Looking at the recent European Innovation Scoreboard, especially if compared to the US and Japan, Europe is lagging behind in number of patents, the working population in the innovative sectors, and research and development (R&D) expenditures. Moreover, the innovation gap with the US and Japan has been widening for the last decade. Improving this state of affairs is one way for Europe to raise its innovative and competitive performance. Taking an innovation[1] from the laboratory to the point at which private commercial investors are willing to fund it as a start-up requires a variety of inputs that can be supplied with in many cases a relatively modest amount of finance. The private sector, acting alone, tends – for sound economic reasons – to produce a rate of throughput that is suboptimal from the public policy viewpoint. Responses to the problem across and outside Europe have taken a wide variety of financial, institutional and organizational approaches. Many programmes have been initiated over the last four to five years.

Being resource efficient and effective in performing R&D start-up conversions is a challenging task and there are many pitfalls. The European Commission is committed to promoting the exchange of experience, ideas and good practice through projects undertaken in the Finance, Innovation and Technology initiative. More in particular, in 2000 the European Commission launched several initiatives in support of sharing and building good practice in university spin-out programmes and academic entrepreneurship – both cornerstones of an innovative European economy. This chapter gives an overview of the main outcomes of some of the Pilot Action of Excellence on Innovative Start-Ups (PAXIS) and Gate2Growth projects, including good practice cases from several European countries and a summary of findings from workshops and conferences which are available on the Gate2Growth website (www.Gate2Growth.com).

2. AN AGENDA FOR A MORE ENTREPRENEURIAL AND INNOVATIVE EUROPE

Within the scope of this concluding chapter it is not possible to cover all the issues considered to determine the European agenda on incubation, technology transfer, intellectual property (IP) management issues, equity financing or fostering an entrepreneurial culture. Therefore, the scope of this chapter is limited to the importance of knowledge generation and the commercialization of research – in other words, technology transfer and spin-out activity – for the Lisbon agenda, that is, propelling the competitiveness and growth of the European economy.

2.1 Generation of Knowledge and Exploitation of IP

First, there is a need to focus on the generation of knowledge before its exploitation: Europe lags behind the US in both. However, the focus on exploitation of research results should not detract from the need to fund 'useless' science (that is, basic research where commercial applications are at least initially unclear) – this was in particular the domain of the public sector. Second, there is a need for patenting, because patents are used mainly to exclude others from using the same invention. It is essential to ensure that there is no prior disclosure of the idea in any form by the inventor because this would constitute prior art, which would prevent filing. The main purpose of a patent is to provide a negotiating position from which to arrange licensing and cross-licensing deals. It is generally useful to have a person who is the link between the patent attorney and the in-house scientists. It is also advisable to keep abreast of third party applications.

There are many issues relating to patent management in general and organizations' solution to spin-out funding problems. Traditionally the technology transfer mechanism has been licensing, that is, not transferring intellectual property rights, but spin-outs and associated equity investments are becoming increasingly important (see Box 13.1: Fraunhofer Patent Centre versus VenTraTec). VC funding is established partly because

---

BOX 13.1   FRAUNHOFER PATENT CENTRE

- the Centre manages the IPR for the national network of *Fraunhofer Institute for Applied Research.*
- provides a professional patent services for clients from outside the FhG.
- IP from FhG inventions belongs to the FhG, the centre is non-profit-making.
- setting up a separate company, *VenTra Tec*, to support spin-out companies for a more entrepreneurial atmosphere and to build better relationships with potential investors of venture capital.
- local VCs have shown considerable interest in investing in the new company, and in the projects that emerge from it.

(http://www.pst.fhg.de/)

---

of the realization that technology transfer requires increasingly a more proactive approach, involving the provision of additional services such as virtual management, patent portfolio and business plan management.

2.2   Increasing Needs for an Entrepreneurial Mindset and Private Equity

Entrepreneurial activity: a cultural change

Many reports have studied structural obstacles to entrepreneurship within many European universities. Introducing an entrepreneurial culture inside a university is a long process and requires substantial reorganization from the bottom up: individual departments are given more independence in exchange for taking on more responsibility in raising external funds for research projects. A number of universities have implanted entrepreneurial values deep into the structures of their organization, for example by making individual research units compete for funding, or by 'embedding' business development executives within faculties with a view to extracting more quickly ideas worthy of commercial consideration. Strong leadership at the top of the university is essential if such wide-ranging cultural changes are to be pushed through. A top-down approach enabled the programme's main features (such as autonomy and fund-raising) to be 'internalized' within the university's normal bureaucratic procedures. Essentially, European universities belong to one of four categories: the 'vertical', or traditional model, the matrix model, the matrix model with services and the technopole. Many are striving to implement the last model, where the university consists mainly of autonomous research units competing for funding both from the university itself and from outside sources.

Fostering an entrepreneurial environment involves managing (incubation and spin-out) programmes along those lines, but also requires good-quality project in-flow from increased entrepreneurial awareness among researchers and strong links with business partners, including financiers, who could add value to projects in the form of specific expertise.

Commonly the main purpose of supporting spin-outs is to sustain the vigour of a commercially oriented R&D organization. However, the generation of revenue, staff motivation, the development of equipment that has wider commercial applications and finally, marketing value, are all valid secondary motivations. Also, attracting the right management team is crucial and, if this could be achieved, attracting finance is less of a problem.

The finance gap

The 'financing gap' of classic university spin-outs with regard to classic venture capital shows little sign of narrowing. If anything, the large sums of money raised by venture capital funds on the back of the dot.com bubble mean that average investment sizes will be driven up simply through the availability of management time not increasing proportionally. This does not work in favour of facilitating access to first-round investment funding for university spin-offs that are generally very small. The reaction to this continuing 'gap' has been for organizations to establish their own seed or pre-seed funds. The question then arises whether these seed funds will be any more successful than straightforward technology transfer offices at paving the way for external venture capitalists to enter into the capital of university spin-outs.

Now that the pendulum of venture capitalists' favour has swung back towards traditional technology companies (including spin-outs), the sector is seeking to achieve a more balanced business. However, it was all the more important that companies demonstrate technical expertise, appropriate incentive structures for staff and, most importantly, previous management experience. The supply of pre-seed finance and the provision of expert services are key areas where support was needed if more people were to be encouraged to set up their own businesses.

Also, there is an acute need for strong linkages (a real 'highway') between the R&D community and the venture capital industry and a need for the public sector to play the key role of broker between the two. It is our belief, however, that venture capitalists are only going to invest in the very small proportion of projects that meet their stringent investment criteria: a strong management team, an identifiable customer need, global potential, a defensible competitive position and the potential to return (at least) 10 times their initial investment.

3. STIMULATING TECHNOLOGY TRANSFER AND SPIN-OUT PROGRAMMES

European technology transfer today shows similarities with an emerging industry: many valuable product ideas; a highly fragmented landscape; lack of critical mass; wide disparities in terms of performances; and developing practices. 'Technology transfer' defines the process of transformation of the results of R&D into marketable products or services. When the transformation takes place and tech transfer is decided, collaboration between the research organization and industry is established, or the technology is licensed or a new company is created (for example, spin-out). But there are many issues involved. Not only do the education and research budgets dwarf the proceeds from technology transfer, and the management of technology transfer often suffers from major deficiencies, but once technology transfer is decided it is usually very unclear whether the IP rights rest with the corporation or with the research organization, or what the aim of the technology transfer is (for instance to maximize profits or the number of spin-outs?).

Spin-out programmes in Europe are characterized by a wide variety of institutional contexts and cultural factors, such as the widespread entrepreneurship and organic networks linking researchers and financiers in the US – a factor that is crucially important. None the less, the average research income from industry in both Europe and the US is 7 per cent and research has shown that the US is not necessarily ahead of Europe on research output in terms of cash invested. In any case, spin-outs are still the exception rather than the norm: licensing and industrial R&D are more important and much research just contributes to the state of the art, so its commercial applicability is indirect. Therefore, 'spin-outs' are appropriate for some projects and not others. Yet, having an efficiently managed and sufficiently large spin-out channel is an important aspect of responding to entrepreneurial instincts among researchers.

The following offers some guidelines. First, spin-out programmes must provide administrative, financial, technological, legal and marketing guidance under supervision. Furthermore, programmes ought to make heavy use of strategic business partners, particularly for technological development assistance, establishing distribution channels and recruiting key staff. To give an example, the University of Nottingham cultivates this more

---

BOX 13.2   BUSINESS RESEARCH UNIT, UNIVERSITY OF NOTTINGHAM

- technology transfer office of the university operates as a department of the university.
- TTO deals with all the externally funded research as well as contacts with industry and technology transfer, regional liaison and IP management.
- companies funding research often also fund conversion activities.
- no dedicated investment fund but university may decide to invest in a start-up.
- recent changes to treat projects in a more systematic way.
- create project budget and allocate number of hours from members of the unit to provide targeted services to technology projects.

(http://www.nottingham.ac.uk/ris/)

Source: Gate2Growth Incubator Forum.

---

strategic perspective on the spin-out process using systematization to achieve greater efficiency. The University of Nottingham Business Research Unit (see Box 13.2) 'embeds' technically trained business development executives in target departments such as pharmaceutical sciences, medicine and biosciences to generate a regular flow of business ideas. These interact with other, 'market-facing', business development executives who carry out a market assessment. A major current debate at the university is whether it should concentrate resources on supporting those projects with high-growth prospects or whether it should specifically provide a service to academics and support lifestyle businesses. In the eye of the private equity investor the latter option would clearly be a waste of public money.

Overall, five main financing mechanisms for spin-out programmes are identified, including three external financing solutions (public sources, private sector and funding from the parent institution) and two nominally self-financing ones (royalty/licensing revenues and returns on equity investments). Compared to the US, the informal investor community is much less developed in Europe. Also, each financing system has advantages and disadvantages. For instance, licensing and other forms of industrial collaboration are possibly more important than spin-outs if organizations are interested in long-term funding streams and building relationships with

---

BOX 13.3   TTI, UNIVERSITY OF STUTTGART

– limited company, mainly owned by the University of Stuttgart.
– built on two pillars: technology and starter centres selling services and products to the market and incubation facilities for start-ups ranging from pre-seed to growth stages.
– scientists may establish a technology and starter centre (ITI profit centre) for sideline businesses.
– gives support for book-keeping, billing, legal support and at a cost of 7% of the turnover.
– provides mentoring schemes and incubation facilities (free use of all university facilities for two years).
– yearly stage/pre-market.

(http://www.uni-stuttgart.de/alumni/careerservice/tti.en.php)

---

powerful technology-driven corporations. But also, the local venture capital environment is fundamental: it impacts on the number of serial entrepreneurs and business angels, but also on the pool of experienced management available from people who have received serial funding. As already indicated, to improve the chances of investment and the potential for success of the start-up, spin-out managers need to add product engineering and marketing early, to be prepared for management changes and to invite publicity for the business and technology. In that respect, setting up clusters and (regional) networks might prove to be very effective. Setting up networks also makes technology transfer less dependent on one university or institution. In view of this, the development of effective networking in Europe needs further support and infrastructure.

Relatively small amounts are needed to keep the project alive during the spin-out process; real investment funding should come from external sources. Spin-outs are principally a means of underpinning the 'commercial vitality' of an institution and secondarily, a means of providing staff with proper incentives in the form of a greater variety of career openings. It seems, as the Technology Transfer Initiative (TTI) of the University of Stuttgart for example demonstrates (see Box 13.3), that there are two broad models of spin-out programme development, which hinge upon initial motivations. We shall refer to these as the growth and lifestyle models.

Under the 'growth' model, spin-outs are pursued aggressively as one means of moving university developed ideas quickly and powerfully into the marketplace with an incidental benefit of generating later additional revenue to reinvest in the technology transfer process and for wider university purposes. The ancillary benefit is to stimulate and reinforce entrepreneurial activities and attitudes within the university. Venture capital techniques are applied, such as buying in professional advisory services and insisting on performance-related milestones to trigger continued support. A concerted effort is made to instil the disciplines that will stand the spin-outs in good stead when conducting negotiations with venture capitalists later on. Indeed, the achievement of substantial venture capital funding can sometimes appear to be the main objective within this model. Commercial selection criteria are applied right from the start, even when ideas are being developed in particular faculties. Under the 'lifestyle' model, large-scale and short-term success in commercialization is not the primary objective of spin-outs, and there are little or no revenue expectations.

A lot of university research was needed just to improve the state of the art, from which foundation others could build projects capable of technology transfer. Universities need to champion a change in culture towards bridging the equity gap that needs policy support at the EU and national level.

4.   EUROPEAN SUPPORT MEASURES: RECENT EXPERIENCE AND GOOD PRACTICE

Introducing an entrepreneurial culture inside a university is a long process and requires substantial reorganization from the bottom up. A number of universities have implanted entrepreneurial values deep into the structure of their organization, for example by making individual research units compete for funding, or by embedding business development executives within faculties with a view to extracting more quickly ideas worthy of commercial consideration. Fostering an entrepreneurial environment involves managing (incubation and spin-out) programmes along those lines, but also requires good quality project in-flow from increased entrepreneurial awareness among researchers and strong links with business partners, including financiers, who could add value to projects in the form of specific expertise.

Many reports have studied structural obstacles to entrepreneurship within many European universities. Many of the issues relate to technology transfer and the creation of spin-outs. Essentially, European universities belong to one of four categories: the vertical or traditional model, the matrix model, the matrix model with services and the technopole. Many are striving to implement the latter model, where the university consists mainly of autonomous research units competing for funding both from the

---

BOX 13.4   RHÔNE-ALPES GENOPOLE

– regional innovative technological platforms and programmes for advanced research (science-industry) and spin-off, tech transfer.
– accessible by both public and industrial research.
– programmes in functional genomics for the region and owns the equipment of the technological platforms.
– business is based on collaboration agreements managed by *Foundation Rhône-Alpes Futur*, responsible for hiring the technical personnel.
– research results are exploited in start-ups, joint ventures or platform cooperation.

(http://www.rhone-alpas-genopole.com)

Source: PAXIS.

---

university itself and from outside sources. The Rhône-Alpes Genopole of Grenoble is presented as an example (see Box 13.4). One of the biggest successes of this genopole is ER-GENTECH, an industrial research laboratory pooling together the technological skills and the scientific know-how in the genomic and biotechnology areas of the Emilia-Romagna region and focusing on technology transfer and spin-off creation. In general, science–industry technology platforms are public–private groupings of universities, research centres (laboratories), industries and institutional public actors sharing the common objective to improve applied research and the exploitation of research results, to structure, enhance and develop joint research activities with a sufficient critical mass that enables them to operate on a large scale, and to set the best conditions for the launch of start-ups and the new technology-based firms (NTBFs). Another example, well embedded in the PAXIS network, is the already discussed TTI of the University of Stuttgart.

The European Commission's PAXIS, Gate2Financing and Gate2Growth initiatives were designed precisely to formalize and expedite the exchange of good practice among innovation professionals, including venture capitalists, incubation managers, IP/licensing managers and academic experts. But Europe does more than support networks of excellence and the exchange of good practices. Because professionals involved in technology transfer systematically agree that Europe faces a number of significant challenges concerning the capitalization of new technologies, the European Investment

Fund (EIF), for instance, launched the Technology Transfer Accelerator (TTA) in 2005.

The aim of the TTA is to bridge the gap between research and early-stage financing through a new financing scheme including targeted risk capital and technology investment vehicle linked centres of excellence from different European countries. The TTA vehicles can promote technology transfer taking place inside research organizations in turn for a share of the technology transfer proceeds either in kind (percentage of licensing equity) or in specie. The vehicles can be created for a finite time (for example, project-based or milestone funding) or be evergreen. TTA vehicles can also carry out technology transfer on behalf of the research organizations or scientists, including investment, in return for a share of the technology transfer proceeds. Here TTA takes place outside the research organization. Or, TTA vehicles might fund portfolios of technology transfer projects, contributed by one or more research organizations (or by individual scientists). In return, the contributors receive a stake in the TTA vehicle (dividend/capital). In this case, the TTA vehicle itself corresponds to such a portfolio of projects. In sum, rather then reinventing the wheel through a top-down approach, the TTA is a flexible and agile financial support for independent technology transfer initiatives, taking advantage of existing financial instruments.

5.   CONCLUSION

In sum, spin-outs are only one of several technology transfer mechanisms and definitely not the easiest way of commercializing research and innovation. So far, the dominant traditional technology transfer mechanisms used have been licensing and contract research. But, there is a strong concern that forcing researchers to seek outside funding and industrial research contracts leads to conflicts of interest. Commonly the main purpose of supporting spin-outs is to sustain the vigour of a commercially oriented R&D organization. However, the generation of revenue, staff motivation, the development of equipment that has wider commercial applications and finally, marketing value, are all valid secondary motivations. Also, attracting the right management team is crucial and, if this could be achieved, attracting finance is less of a problem.

In a spin-out programme, support services are essential – often finance is viewed as less important by the end users. Now that the pendulum of venture capitalists' favour has swung back towards traditional technology companies (including spin-outs) apparently the sector is seeking to achieve a more balanced business. It was all the more important that companies demonstrate technical expertise, appropriate incentive structures for staff and, most importantly, previous management experience. The supply of pre-seed finance and the provision of expert services are key areas where support was needed if more people were to be encouraged to set up their own businesses. In other words management support, financial/accounting services and IP management are all possibly more important than direct funding.

The multiplicity of solutions offered to assist the spin-out process partly reflects the fact that European universities or research institutes are long-established, inward-looking and often bureaucratic organizations, structurally dependent on public sector funding. This can be contrasted with the major US universities which have always had to interact with the private sector in order to survive and flourish. In order for European universities to become better at fostering entrepreneurial results for their research, the public sector also needs to change. And things are changing – over the past decade some research institutions employed a number of policy measures to encourage and help spin-offs. These included a 'right to return' to employment at the research institution in the event of failure, interest-free loans to provide entrepreneurs with their 'own' capital necessary to obtain external funding and incubation facilities. Job security, interest-free funding and access to its laboratory facilities might also be instrumental in organizing a syndicate of venture capitalists willing to invest in the spin-out company. On the downside, there could be some tension between technologists/researchers and in-house financiers, in that the former were interested in short-term funding while the latter wanted to maximize long-term returns.

On a more general level, there is a long way to go in order to maximize benefits from university and public research through the creation of spin-outs. Therefore it is necessary to increase efforts in making technology transfer offices more professional. These, before all other parties concerned, should inform academic entrepreneurs and tech start-ups of the differences between potential investment channels and the impact of this on their venture and on how to approach venture capitalists. There is a strong need to revise public policy with regard to the venture capital, including refocusing on small funds and increasing efforts with regard to the business angel community.

NOTES

* An early version of this chapter has been submitted for the PAXIS Manual 2006, www.cordis.lu/paxis.
1. For a definition of 'innovation', see European Commission COM(1995) 688.

Index

Index

spin-outs highly diverse 154, 156–7
variation depending on precise area
  of potential support required
  by spin-out venture 155, 158
QUIBIS, Queen's University
  technology transfer company 154

R&D community and VC industry,
  need for strong linkages between
  178
Ratification 6, 10, 12
rational expectations and perfect
  competitiveness, govern pricing in
  financing rounds 44
research,
  shown that US not necessarily ahead
    of Europe on research output
    179
  value-adding roles for the VCF 120
research institutions, number of policy
  measures to encourage and help
  spin-offs 185
Reynolds, T.L. 80, 83
Rhône-Alpes Genopole of Grenoble
  183
Richardson, M. 51, 56
Rigel 105, 107, 109, 111, 114
Robinson, R.J. 5–6, 8
Roure, J. 60
Route 128 Boston 162
Rushworth, S. 65
Ruud, A. 56

Sahlman, W.A. 124–5, 127
de San José Riestra, A. 60
Sapienza, H.J. 120, 122–3
scale and seed activity, relationship not
  linear 166
Schamp, T. 175
Schoar, A. 47, 56
'screening', number of specific and
  separate activities 9–10
'screening I'. fund documentation is
  vetted 10
'screening II',
  investors conducted introductory
    meetings with VCs but did not
    embark into detail assessment
    10
  LPs and meetings with VCs 5–6

screening of potential VC deals, prior
  experience of investor 170
screening stage, selection criteria cited
  by investors 10
seed capital,
  hard and stony road for both
    investors and governments 174
  how it works and behaviour of
    investment executives 165–6
  most European investors are
    'nimbys' 174
  supply of perceived as problematic
    165
seed capital investment, increasing
  fund size not necessarily a barrier
  to 173
seed investing, mechanism for investors
  to stay at forefront of industry
  developments 168
seed phase of the company, technology
  investors 21
segmentation 50–51, 57–8
'serial' founder, brings more wealth to
  the new venture 93
seven European high-tech regions, 68
  early-stage high-tech investors and
  conjoint analysis 17
Shepherd, D.A. 16
six sequential steps, venture capital
  decision process 3
small and medium-sized enterprises *see*
  SMEs
SMEs 161–2
social capital,
  CBVCs and 108
  relevant when explaining
    internationalization behaviour
    of firms 103
software company B 155, 159, 160
software company C 158–9
software company D, fastest growing
  inner-city-based business in UK
  154–5
software company J. remained small
  154
software company K, grown rapidly
  154–5
software company M 159
software development, labour rather
  than capital-intensive activity 101